MW00444167

Charles Malik, President of the United Nations General Assembly in 1958 and Lebanese Ambassador to the United States and the United Nations in 1945 once said to me, "The fastest way to bring about change is to mobilize women." Women committed to making "the table" prominent in our homes can change the world. Let's go for it.

—Vonette Z. Bright,
Co-Founder, Campus Crusade for Christ

Devi Titus' practical explanation addresses our society's major challenge-broken families. She offers unique and applicable solutions to restoring and maintaining whole families. It is insightful and convicting, in an inspiring way. Both men and women can benefit from it.

—Lois Evans,
A Women of Influence's Woman of the Year,
Senior Vice President of The Urban Alternative
and Wife of Dr. Tony Evans

Devi Titus' remarkable teaching gift is matched by the genius of her creative skill in crafting a message that is made to order for discipling a new generation. If "home is where the heart is formed" as Devi says, a home with a godly atmosphere can influence the hearts of all who enter yours! You and others will benefit from deeper, more meaningful relationships. Mesdames and Sirs everywhere, I recommend this book highly!!

—Dr. Jack W. Hayford,
Chancellor, The King's College and Seminary

We have taught the principles of *The Table Experience* extensively in our church, and we would encourage other church leaders to do the same. *The Table Experience* has led our congregation into a dynamic time of Christ-centered fellowship around their tables that has been both deeply nourishing and powerfully healing. Thanks to Devi Titus' strong teaching and home life expertise, the table has again become a sacred and cherished place of honor, love, serving, and celebration. We are so grateful for Devi helping to recover and renew this thoroughly biblical principle and practice, and would wholeheartedly recommend this book to be read by everyone, everywhere.

—Pastor Dale and Joan Evrist,
New Song Christian Fellowship, Nashville, Tennessee

When the Lord wanted to build a nation, he gathered his people around the Glory Presence Holy Place and the Table of Showbread. When Jesus wanted to prepare the disciples for ministry in His absence, He gathered them around a table. David said when the Lord leads him through the valley; he prepares a table in the presence of our enemies. Devi Titus has received the revelation of the power of the Table as a place of restoration for families, the development of Kingdom principles, and the formation of godly character.

Following the model of the Master who gathered His disciples around a table to prepare them for life in His absence, Devi Titus shares the principles of the table which God uses to build families, strengthen love, and shape character. Prepare to be blessed!

—Dr. Kenneth C. Ulmer, President,
The King's College and Seminary

Devi Titus is passionate about helping families. In *The Table Experience*, she teaches us the importance of coming together to dine and fellowship around the family table. You and your family will be forever changed by this book as you realize the importance of spending quality time together.

—Joni Lamb, Co-Founder,
Daystar Television Network

THE **TABLE** EXPERIENCE

DISCOVER WHAT CREATES DEEPER,
MORE MEANINGFUL RELATIONSHIPS

DEVI TITUS

THE **TABLE** EXPERIENCE

DISCOVER WHAT CREATES DEEPER,
MORE MEANINGFUL RELATIONSHIPS

DEVI TITUS

Oviedo, Florida

THE TABLE EXPERIENCE
by Devi Titus

Published by HigherLife Development Services, Inc.
2342 Westminster Terrace
Oviedo, FL 32765
407-563-4806
www.ahigherlife.com

All rights reserved. No portion of this book may be reproduced, stored in a retrieval system, or transmitted in any form or by any means—electronic, mechanical, photocopy, recording, scanning, or other—except for brief quotations in critical reviews or articles, without the prior written permission of the publisher.

All Scripture quotations, unless otherwise indicated, are taken from the NEW AMERICAN STANDARD BIBLE®, Copyright © 1960, 1962, 1963, 1968, 1971, 1972, 1973, 1975, 1977, 1995 by The Lockman Foundation. Used by permission.

Scripture quotations marked NIV are taken from HOLY BIBLE: NEW INTERNATIONAL VERSION®. Copyright © 1973, 1978, 1984 by International Bible Society. Used by permission of Zondervan Publishing House. All rights reserved.

Scripture quotations marked NLT are taken from the Holy Bible, New Living Translation, Copyright © 1996, 2004. Used by permission of Tyndale House Publishers, Inc., Wheaton, IL 60189. All rights reserved.

Scripture quotations marked ICB are taken from the INTERNATIONAL CHILDREN'S BIBLE®. Copyright © 1986, 1988, 1999 by Thomas Nelson, Inc. Used by permission. All rights reserved.

Copyright © 2009 by Devi Titus
All rights reserved

ISBN: 978-1-935245-13-1

Cover Design: Judith McKittrick Wright

First Edition
09 10 11 12 - 5 4 3 2 1
Printed in the United States of America

Dedication

To Larry, my lover and my friend, my spiritual
inspiration, and my personal motivator. You believe
that I can do anything and allow me to try.

To our children, Trina Titus Lozano and Dr. Aaron P. Titus,
and their families. Your example and life-choices bring me
great reward. Thank you for all the dirty dishes you helped
to wash when we invited people to our table. You willingly
served our guests and shared our affections with others.

To my mother, a wise woman indeed, who continues to pour
her wisdom and principles into me. Mom and Dad truly
lived practical Christianity—loving God by loving others.

To every person who has sat at our table and took
pleasure in our table experience—whether we shared
a meal, played a game, or engaged in meaningful
discussions. May your lives continue to be enriched
as you enjoy the table experience with others.

Contents

Acknowledgments

I WANT TO EXPRESS MY deep gratitude to four very special people who have been a vital part of this project.

Larry Titus, my husband—you believed in me. Words seem weak to fully express my love and appreciation for your encouragement and patience as I pressed to this deadline. Our photo albums are full of pictures of our precious family around our table. It's because of you that I can write these principles. Thank you for sitting at the head of our table.

Jennifer Stair, my editor—you polished me. Your communication abilities are amazing, and I loved working with you. Hearing the voices of your young children in the background while we talked on the phone reminded me that not only were you doing what you do so well, polishing my manuscript, but your heart as a mom was capturing the message of this book.

Joy and Jennifer, my partners in this mission—you propelled me with your generosity. Your support for this project will forever be remembered. I am deeply grateful. Because of you, multitudes will experience deeper, more meaningful relationships.

Keep it simple.
Make it pretty.

Chapter 1

What Are We Missing?

A man was giving a big dinner, and he invited many; and at the dinner hour he sent his slave to say to those who had been invited, "Come; for everything is ready now."

—Luke 14:16

IN THE SPRING OF 2000, I was invited to be the keynote speaker at a women's conference in Fresno, California. The general audience included more than four thousand women who had gathered for a time of worship, renewal, and biblical teaching.

I can honestly say that this women's conference was one of the most awesome events I have ever been part of. From beginning to end, our time together was God-honoring. The details of the event were well planned; everything from registration to the closing celebration flowed seamlessly. During the worship team's sessions, the presence of God was clearly evident. People worshiped freely and loved one another compassionately. The event had been covered in prayer, and it was a truly profound experience.

Often, when you have participated in that kind of God-filled event, whether at a church service or conference or retreat, you come home feeling excited and filled with the joy of the Lord. This time was different for me, however. For some reason, I came home from the conference feeling frustrated and empty. It had nothing to do with this excellent conference. But something was gnawing at me—a nagging sense that something was wrong.

What Are We Missing?

The day after coming home from California, I took my Bible and went to my "Yada chair"—a special place I have set aside in my home where the Lord and I meet on an intimate level.[1] My heart was heavy and burdened, so I asked God to help me understand why.

I thought about what we speakers tend to do at Christian conferences. We teach what the Bible says about obedience, forgiveness, emotional issues, family matters, being fully committed to Christ, and so on. We seek God's direction and select which of these topics will be appealing and helpful to a specific audience.

But over the years, I began to sense that somehow we weren't addressing the underlying issue. Conference attendees would enjoy the heartfelt worship and solid Bible teaching, but then they would go home to families that were broken and hurting. For some reason, the biblical messages they were hearing in these conferences, and even in their own churches, were not making a lasting difference in their lives and family relationships.

A few months earlier, my husband, Larry, and I had heard George Barna, one of the world's foremost statisticians on Christian faith and culture, give the sobering results of a survey of church-attending families in America. Barna's research revealed the divorce rate among churchgoing families was now *higher* than families who did not attend church.[2]

That statistic burrowed deep into my heart. At the time, Larry and I had already spent more than thirty years in pastoral ministry. We had made many sacrifices for the sake of the church and the gospel and the kingdom of God. So when I heard that the marriages of churchgoers were more likely to end in divorce, I thought, *What have Larry and I spent the past thirty years of our lives doing?* My soul seemed to sink. *If the divorce rate is higher for churchgoers, then why would we encourage anyone to go to church?*

I asked the Lord, "What has happened in the thirty years that Larry and I have been pastoring? Something is terribly wrong in families across America, and things are getting worse, not better. We have megachurches filled with tens of thousands of people every Sunday, and yet families are becoming more fragmented and marriages are more likely to end, despite *higher* church attendance! What is happening, Lord? There's something we're missing! But what?"

"What is happening, Lord? There's something we're missing! But what?"

One Small Plate

I couldn't help but think of the parallel of the disintegration of the American family and the disintegration of the space shuttle *Columbia*. Let me take you back to February 1, 2003...

NASA flight STS-107, the space shuttle *Columbia*, began her reentry into the atmosphere after a successful mission. Suddenly, the craft's external heat sensors picked up a spike in temperature. Communication with ground control became staticky and jumbled.

"Mission control, mission control, this is space shuttle *Columbia*. Please verify onboard external heat senso—"

3

The transmission suddenly broke off.

"Columbia, this is mission control. Please repeat. We lost your transmission. Please repeat. Over."

No response.

"*Columbia* STS-107, this is mission control. Do you copy? Over."

Still no response. Because at that moment, flight STS-107 was disintegrating in the earth's atmosphere. All seven astronauts onboard were lost.

The nation was stunned, and the entire space shuttle program was immediately grounded. A panel of top investigators began poring over the evidence, trying to discover what had caused this sudden, unforeseen national tragedy. In the same way, I feel that the condition of the American family is a sudden, unforeseen national tragedy.

In the early days of the accident investigation, like a still, small voice crying in the wilderness of the multitude of theories, one lone investigator posed what sounded like an absurd question: "Is it possible that one tiny heat shield tile might have caused the entire shuttle to be utterly destroyed?"

"Impossible!" was the resounding conclusion of the world's finest scientific minds. They reasoned that they had been flying the shuttle for more than seventeen years without mishap, and the failure of *one small tile* could not possibly bring down the entire spacecraft.

This is how I felt—like the small voice crying from my chair, alone in my inquiry. *What is causing the demise of the family and causing it to disintegrate?*

Yet only by the insistent voice of that one accident investigator was the culprit exposed. Perhaps that could be me. *Maybe if I pursue an answer to my question, "What are we missing?" I can bring insight to what can make our families stronger,* I thought.

Finally, the investigative panel made the announcement: "The tragic disaster of the destruction of NASA space shuttle *Columbia*, flight STS-107, was due to a small fissure in a protective heat shield tile that allowed a tiny crack to grow until the buildup of pressure and heat caused several protective plates to break away. During reentry, these plates hit the leading edge of the wing, causing the spacecraft to disintegrate in the earth's atmosphere."

One structural weakness only a few centimeters wide caused a catastrophe and shut down a multibillion-dollar federal program run by the most brilliant minds in the world. One tiny, overlooked crack that festered and grew and destroyed lives. One small ceramic tile, designed to be a key ally of the spacecraft and her occupants, its sole purpose to protect them from the destructive heat of the atmosphere. Once that tile was pried away, chaos began its course. That tiny crack in that one little tile took down the spacecraft and shut down the entire program. One small plate.

I thought, *Is it possible that one small function in our homes, if neglected, could end up causing the destruction of the entire institution of family? If so, what is it?*

One Little Word That Refocused My Life

I didn't get an answer from God that day. In fact, it wasn't the next day or even the next week. Several months went by, and I was still searching Scripture and asking God, "What are we missing?"

Then one day, as I was doing housework, one little word suddenly popped into my mind: *table.*

I didn't think much about it at the time; after all, the word *table* didn't seem like something spiritual. I didn't get goose bumps or chills or feel like it was the Holy Spirit speaking to me. It just was a thought.

A few days later, the word popped back into my mind.
Table.
Table? *Hmm. Table. Okay, that's nice.*

In the morning, the word came back to me again.

Table.

This continued for a couple of days. Finally, curious about that word and why it kept coming to my mind, I called a friend who had Bible software on her computer. "Would you please search the Bible for the word *table*, and see what comes up?" I asked her.

The next day she printed out and brought me several pages of Scripture references from Genesis to Revelation that included the word *table*. I was amazed at how many verses there were about the table! And her list didn't include synonyms, such as *eat with, dine with, banquet* and so on; she had only searched for the word *table*.

I couldn't believe that something referenced this many times in Scripture had been so overlooked. In thirty-five years of preaching, my husband had never preached a sermon on the table. I had never heard a sermon on the radio or on television about the table. I had never read a book that explained God's principle of the table. How could we have missed the importance of something God mentioned so often in His Word? Was this the message God wanted me to share with His people?

I started digging into Scripture, eagerly searching for answers, and I was amazed at what I found about God's principle of the table. Here are just a few of the scriptures I discovered:

- "Make a *table*" (Ex. 25:23).

- "Put the bread of the Presence on the *table* before Me at all times" (Ex. 25:30).

- "They made from pure gold the articles for the *table*—its dishes, cups, bowls and pitchers" (Ex. 37:16 NIV).

- "You shall eat at my *table* regularly" (2 Sam. 9:7).

- "For the rest of his life [he] ate regularly at the king's *table*" (2 Kings 25:29 NIV).

- "You prepare a *table* before me in the presence of my enemies" (Ps. 23:5).

- "Your wife shall be like a fruitful vine in your house, your children like olive plants around your *table*" (Ps. 128:3).

- "She has prepared her food, she has mixed her wine; she has also set her *table*" (Prov. 9:2).

- "When evening came, Jesus was reclining *at the table* with His twelve disciples" (Matt. 26:20).

- "Afterward, He appeared to the eleven themselves as they were reclining at the *table*" (Mark 16:14).

- "Just as My Father has granted me a kingdom, I grant you that you may eat and drink at my *table* in the kingdom" (Luke 22:29–30).[3]

As I began to uncover the significance of the table in Scripture—from the tabernacle in ancient times all the way through the kingdom of God after the end of this world—I was surprised to learn how many important events and teachings and miracles took place while people were dining together. Perhaps this table experience was the very revelation in God's Word that we had been missing!

> As I began to uncover the significance of the
> table in Scripture...I was surprised to learn
> how many important events and teachings
> and miracles took place while people were
> dining together.

I am convinced that God has given us all the truth we need to know for life in the Holy Bible. In fact, whenever the media proudly asserts that contemporary research has "discovered" a new truth, we find that principle already laid out for us in the pages of Scripture. So as I began to see how often the Bible speaks about the importance of the table, I decided to broaden my research to see if historical and scientific research would confirm what I was uncovering about what creates deeper, more meaningful relationships.

It Starts at Home

In his exhaustive, six-volume commentary *The Decline and Fall of the Roman Empire,* written in 1788, English historian Edward Gibbon observes five root causes that contributed to the downfall of one of the greatest empires in the world.[4] Gibbon's principles are widely recognized by historians as applying to all great civilizations. The most significant cause of a civilization's fall, interestingly, is not a lack of military strength or political savvy. The most crushing blow to an empire does not come from outside forces trying to conquer and dominate it. No, Gibbon says, the foundation of a great civilization crumbles when it is weakened from within. And what comes first on his list of contributors to an empire's downfall? "The undermining of the dignity and sanctity of the home, which is the basis for human society."[5]

The greatest empires in the world were defeated, not because of someone else's military or political strength, but because they became vulnerable when they stopped paying attention to what was happening at home. The home is not just a physical structure where a family dwells. It's not just the return address on your mail or the place where you park your car at night. God designed the home to be a central part of our lives. The home is to be a nurturing place where family members build healthy relationships with one another, learning and laughing and growing together, and building a sense of identity and community from which a society is formed.

Whether it is a tent or a mansion, a dwelling of any kind becomes a home when people spend time together there. We all know the cliché, "Home is where the heart is." I like to use a variation of this statement passed to me by a friend: "Home is where the heart is *formed.*" There is something very dynamic about the home in relationship to the human heart. In the home, our hearts can either be hurt or hardened because of what we have experienced, or they can be strengthened and made to become secure and sensitive because of what happens in the home.

Gibbon observes that when families no longer spend time at home, the foundation of the society begins to crumble. Yet all too often in America, our homes have ceased to be the center of our family's activities. Between work and school and Little League and piano lessons and community service and, yes, even church activities, many families are no longer at home! We rush to leave our homes early in the morning and come back late at night, exhausted and ready to climb into bed. In many families, driving through fast-food restaurants and grabbing dinner on the go has replaced spending time together in the evenings, gathered face-to-face around the table, eating dinner and talking with one another.

As I reflected on the importance of the home, I thought, *If the home is the basis of human society, then is it possible that the table is the basis of human stability?* Could it be that the table experience—the simple act of eating meals together regularly at the family table—is absolutely vital to the long-term health and stability of our families and our society?

A growing excitement ignited my curiosity. The more I researched, the more confirmation I discovered.

> Could it be that the table experience—the simple act of eating meals together regularly at the family table—is absolutely vital to the long-term health and stability of our families and our society?

Smarter, Stronger, Healthier, and Happier

Award-winning documentary filmmaker and journalist Miriam Weinstein has spent many years honing her research skills on a variety of subjects. In her book *The Surprising Power of Family Meals,* she draws on studies from psychology, education, nutrition, and sociology regarding the cultural phenomenon of family meals. Her thorough study of this subject led Weinstein to the surprising and bold conclusion that eating family meals together is a "magic bullet" that dramatically improves "the quality of your daily life, your children's chances of success in the world, your family's health, [and] our values in society."[6] In the subtitle of her book and on her Web site, Weinstein concludes that eating family meals makes us "smarter, stronger, healthier, and happier."[7]

As I pondered those words, I realized that they perfectly describe the whole person—body, mind, soul, spirit. We are *smarter* (in our minds), *stronger* (in our spirits), *healthier* (in our bodies), and *happier* (in our souls) when we eat meals together at the dinner table with our families and loved ones. Doesn't it make sense that God, who created us as mind-spirit-body-soul beings, would also provide an opportunity for us to nourish all four dimensions on a daily basis? And if so, is it possible that God Himself is present with us in a special way as we gather together at the family table to nourish our bodies, minds, souls, and spirits?

Weinstein thinks so. Although her book focuses on the physical and emotional benefits of family meals, she notes that as she observed and participated in dinner experiences with various families, she made an interesting discovery: eating family meals at the table also seems to have a unique spiritual significance. She observes, "Each time we say grace, we are including another presence at our table—God comes to dinner."[8]

> Eating family meals at the table also seems to
> have a unique spiritual significance.

For years, I have taught and demonstrated to young women the importance of preparing the table in their homes, even when they are single. At the time, I did not fully understand the biblical principle that I now know; I just knew that setting the table was important. When I was a young pastor's wife, the high school and college-age girls in our church loved hanging out at my home. Whenever the girls visited, I would offer them something to eat, such as a snack of peanut butter and apples, soup, cookies—whatever I had on hand. Sometimes it was as simple as toast and jam.

These girls loved sitting at my table. Back then, Larry and I did not have much, so we just used what we had. Our chairs did not match the color of the décor, and my small plastic-topped table was always covered with a tablecloth—not because I was trying to be fancy, but because the table was ugly! I would set a plate and a napkin at each place, although we were crowded. The napkins were made of cloth because on my weekly budget, I could not afford paper napkins. (I reasoned that cloth napkins could be washed and reused.)

The girls loved the cloth napkins. Sometimes I folded them in origami-like fancy folds, and other times I tied them in simple knots. They were fascinated! We often finished our time at the table with the girls trying to recreate the napkin fold they had disassembled. They would linger for a long time after sharing our simple snack together; often it seemed like they dreaded leaving. These hippie young women of the 1970s were not my family, but they loved to be in my home because they felt welcome and valued while they were at my table.

A Supernatural Presence at the Table

Contemporary psychological and sociological discoveries are shedding light on the very same things I have been practicing in my home for years, even though God did not reveal the table principle in the Bible to me until recently. The results of several studies are beginning to confirm that families who take time to eat together at the dinner table do better in every area—body, mind, soul, and spirit. This just goes to show that God's Word is true, and modern research is simply confirming the truths God has already given us in His Word.

Not only are we encouraged, enhanced, and enriched by the presence of our loved ones during the dinner experience, but I strongly believe that there is another presence—a supernatural presence—at the table, whether we invite Him or not. When we set aside time to gather as a family around the table, the presence of God will meet us there, and He is able to do in the human heart what we cannot do.

It makes no difference whether your dinner table is set for one or two or twelve. God's presence at the table does not depend on the number of people, the quality of the food, or the presentation of the dishes or table setting. As we will explore in more detail in later chapters, He promises that if we set the table, He will meet with us and dine with us, and we will experience intimate fellowship with Him there. God's supernatural presence will reveal the secret potential in every person who is seated at the table.

> God's supernatural presence will reveal the secret potential in every person who is seated at the table.

Fireworks of Truth

As I continued my study of the table experience, as presented in Scripture and confirmed by scientific research, the hidden potential of eating meals together began emerging in wondrous bursts of insight, like fireworks of truth lighting the darkness.

I asked questions, such as:

- How can eating meals together help a family avoid the dismal statistics about divorce?

- In what ways are families compromising God's design for the dinner experience in our homes, perhaps without realizing it?

- Is there anything wrong with grabbing food on the go or eating wherever we want to in the house, or does God's design demonstrate some sort of an approach for eating family meals?

- God could have created our bodies so that we never had to eat at all, or perhaps we'd only need to eat once a month, or even yearly. Why, then, did He make our bodies in such a way that eating is a daily need—even three times a day?

- Why does Jesus invite us to dine with Him in Revelation 3:20? What is it about the dinner experience that makes it such a meaningful encounter?

- Is our dinner "togetherness" experience with Jesus meant to be only a one-time activity, or does He intend us to continue to dine with Him regularly?

- Is it possible that the dinner experience—the simple act of eating together regularly at the table—has the potential of unleashing a supernatural work in our families that will form the lasting character and stability and life transformation we have been missing?

My research led to the stunning answer to those questions. I learned why the table experience is completely life-altering. I learned a truth that transcends cultures and history: since ancient times, the table has been a central part of life and was designed by God Himself for a specific, ongoing purpose. What I learned from my study of the table changed the entire focus of my life. And in these pages, I hope to stir up your understanding so that you, too, can grow in your own study of what I like to call the "table principle."

If we want to preserve and protect our homes and marriages and families, if we want to enjoy the hidden potential we have been missing, and if we want to restore a foundational principle that God Himself established thousands of years ago, then it's time for us to set the table!

> Is it possible that the table experience—the
> simple act of eating together regularly at
> the table—has the potential of unleashing a
> supernatural work in our families?

As I will show you in this book, I am convinced that God is revealing to us the secret potential of eating meals together. As we learn and apply this principle, the supernatural presence of God will meet us at the table, and the table experience will nourish and heal our hearts, deepen our relationships, and strengthen our homes and churches and communities, and even our nation and our world!

Table Reflections

1. What is the beginning of the eventual fall of a great empire according to Edward Gibbon?

2. What is the home intended to be in relationship to society?

3. Which Bible verses about the table spoke to you the most?

4. What are four expected results of eating meals together, as noted by academic research, according to author Miriam Weinstein?

5. Complete this sentence: Home is where the heart is _____.

Part 1

The Table Is a Place of Purpose

Chapter 2

A Place at God's Table

Place the Bread of the Presence on the table to remain before me at all times.

—Exodus 25:30 NLT

S EVERAL YEARS AGO, MY husband and I purchased, along with an investor, an eight-thousand-square-foot historical home to become the site of a ministry called the Mentoring Mansion. This grand edifice would serve as my guest home, where twice a month, a group of eight ladies would sign up to spend four days with me learning how to make their homes places of love and peace. My goal during these Home Mentoring Intensives was to equip these women to restore the dignity and sanctity of the home.[1]

Larry had recently resigned as senior pastor of our local congregation and, after thirty plus years in the pastorate, had decided to pursue a unique ministry. This transition was very difficult for me to accept. I could not imagine life without my husband being the pastor of a local church. Serving alongside my husband was my platform to do what was my passion—teaching and training women to reach their greatest potential.

As the senior pastor's wife, I loved ministering to women in our congregations, helping them to be fruitful and fulfilled in all aspects of their lives. I invented creative, nonreligious venues to do this. Rarely did I have traditional settings for ministry like a Bible study in a church classroom. When I taught a Bible study, I usually arranged to meet in a living room or a country club, in order to reach as many women as possible with the transforming truth of God's Word. The Mentoring Mansion would be my new creative venue to train multitudes of women to be confident and godly in their homes and professions, using the curriculum I developed called *The Home Experience: Making Your Home a Sanctuary of Love and a Haven of Peace.*[2]

The historic home we purchased, built in 1915, was a stunning structure. However, it had not been well maintained, so its beauty was clouded by outdated décor. As friends and family caught the vision for the Mentoring Mansion, we teamed together to make this home a bright spot in the neighborhood. A local high school football team put in new landscaping, a neighbor installed exterior lighting, and men, women, and children who supported our ministry were mobilized like ants setting out to build a colony. Working together, we raked and scraped, cleaned and steamed. The transformation was profound, as if the clock had been turned back to the early century, the time when this incredible structure had been built.

With the furniture in place, the bedrooms prepared, and the living areas sparkling clean, my first guests arrived. I was so excited to finally begin my twenty-year dream—to bring women into a home to learn about the home. I would be like a surrogate mom to these precious women for four days, teaching them important skills in homemaking and honoring God in their homes. What a privilege! Maybe, just maybe, I could be an instrument to begin a movement in our nation that would strengthen families and create tools for lasting marriages.

In the process of preparing the Mentoring Mansion for our first guests, I noticed a periodic drip coming from the upstairs bathroom showerhead. But because I would only have guests using this shower eight days per month, I decided that I could live with the drip. As soon as my guests departed, I turned off the main water supply to the upstairs tub, and for several months, that minor effort was sufficient to prolong my need to make this repair.

Our cash flow for the Mentoring Mansion was limited, so I chose to do other things with my money. I bought colorful placemats and dishes—things that were much prettier than plumbing pipes—to brighten the appearance of the home. Yet the persistent drip in the upstairs shower continued and soon could not be tolerated. We replaced the shower nozzle, but that did not stop the drip. Then we replaced the washers on the faucets. Again, no success.

Finally, I called a plumber. He opened the access panel from inside the adjoining closet and carefully examined the plumbing pipes servicing the tub and shower. After assessing the situation, he told me, "Ma'am, you have a much bigger problem than a small drip in your shower. If you want to avoid a worse outcome later, what you really need to do is replace the entire tub, drain, faucets, and showerhead." I thought, *This is just a small drip. I bet he's just saying that because he wants to make a lot of money.* I did not follow his advice. I didn't think this small drip was a big deal—we could live with it.

We did live with it for a number of months, until one day I noticed a small brown circle on our newly painted kitchen ceiling. It looked as if someone had thrown a water balloon and popped it on the ceiling just to the side of the kitchen table. I couldn't figure out how in the world the ceiling became soiled. I was trying to solve the problem from looking at the surface. But the problem was not on the surface; it was coming from somewhere much deeper—and much higher.

I had ignored the expert. I had rationalized that the problem could be contained as a small drip in the tub. I was wrong.

The dark circle on the ceiling became larger. The plaster bubbled and cracked, and the crown molding began to pull away from the edge of the ceiling. After several weeks (I'm a slow learner), I thought, *This must be water coming from somewhere.* I brought in a handyman to repair the kitchen ceiling because the stain was becoming unsightly. He surveyed the situation and concluded, "Lady, I cannot repair the ceiling until you repair your plumbing."

I replied, "Oh, we don't have a plumbing problem. It's no big deal—just a small drip in the upstairs shower. Here, let me show you."

He said politely, "You don't have to show me, ma'am. I'm sorry to have to tell you that your small drip has become a much bigger issue."

Because I ignored the advice of an expert and was unwilling to pay the price to repair the small leak in a proper way, I now had to replace the complete jetted bathtub and shower, tile, and enclosure, in addition to the kitchen ceiling.

So it can be in our lives. We often ignore little things, even when others who know more than us point out these warning signs. Then, too late, we discover that these "little things" left untended have caused significant damage. Because we do not realize the long-term impact of our decisions, we prolong the important for the sake of convenience or self-interests.

Can something as simple as neglecting family meals at the table bring to us regret and disappointment in our lives? If this essential need in our home is left unattended, will there be greater repair to deal with later—a repair that did not need to be made in the first place? This is a question we will explore as we search God's Word for His truth about the importance of the table.

> Can something as simple as neglecting family meals at the table bring to us regret and disappointment in our lives?

In this chapter, I'm going to take you on a simple journey through the Bible, highlighting a few scriptures that reveal the secret potential of eating meals together. As you read, I pray that the Holy Spirit will bring to your mind other scriptures, and you'll start seeing the many facets of this truth burst forth like fireworks, the way I did when I studied this subject.

You see, as you begin to understand this revelation, it becomes a conviction. The truth God reveals to you enters your heart, and when you are convinced, it becomes yours. So as you take ownership of the truth of the table principle, I pray that the table experience—this seemingly insignificant act of coming together to share a meal at the table—will transform your life and your family forever.

The Table God Designed

The first time the word *table* is used in the Bible is in Exodus 25.[3] In this chapter, God gave Moses very detailed instructions about the furniture to be placed in the tabernacle, the first official gathering place for His people. During this time in Old Testament history, God was in the process of transitioning His relationship with His people. From this point on, He would relate differently than He did in the book of Genesis. From the garden of Eden to Mount Sinai, God had appeared at will to walk and talk with certain people at specific times of His choosing. But after the Exodus, God revealed to Moses that He would change the way He related to humankind—He wanted them to create a dwelling place where God's presence would continually abide among His people. God said to Moses, "Construct a sanctuary for Me, that I may dwell among them" (Ex. 25:8).

Think of God as the architect and Moses as the general contractor. The architect has the vision and creates the concept and layout of the building. He decides what the building will look like and what kinds of materials to use. Then, after the building has been designed, the general contractor hires skilled craftsmen and builds the structure according to the architect's blueprints. In Exodus 25, God gave Moses a blueprint for the tabernacle, something that had never existed, so He described very elaborate details, down to each item's material and size and design.

The first piece of furniture God instructed Moses to build for the tabernacle was the ark of the covenant (Ex. 25:10–22). The ark was, to put it in very simple terms, an ornate container for the presence of God. This rectangular box was overlaid with gold and had carved cherubim on either side. Although the design for the ark was intricate and very meaningful, the structure itself was not seen by the public, except when it was carefully transported by a select group of priests to the next destination in Israel's journey through the wilderness. Yet when it was in its proper place in the tabernacle, the ark of the covenant was hidden behind a thick veil in an area of the tabernacle called the Holy of Holies, where God's presence dwelled. The veil separated people from the presence of God; only the high priest could go behind the veil on behalf of the people—only one day a year, and only after bringing an acceptable sacrifice.

The next piece of furniture God told Moses to build for the tabernacle is the table of showbread. Remember, God was just giving Moses the design at this time; the table doesn't actually exist yet. In fact, to the best of my knowledge, none of the items in the tabernacle had ever existed before in these dimensions, which is why God had to give Moses such detailed descriptions.

Although some very early tables were made and used by the Egyptians, they were little more than metal or stone platforms used to keep objects off the floor. They were not used for seating people. So I imagine that when God gave Moses these very important detailed descriptions of the table He wanted in the tabernacle, Moses could likely imagine such an ornate piece of furniture, since he was reared in Egyptian royal opulence. However, the table for the tabernacle was different. It was taller and made with unique materials in a different way than the Egyptian tables. God was designing something unique and new. The table that Moses built for the tabernacle was the height that food could be served from or that chairs could fit under, much like the tables that we use today.

You shall make a table of acacia wood, two cubits long and one cubit wide and one and a half cubits high. (v. 23)

I grew up going to church, and over the years I had heard several people teach about the tabernacle. I remembered seeing drawings and charts of what the items in the tabernacle looked like and how they symbolized various aspects of our relationship with God—but to be honest, I had always kind of passed it by. I would think, *Let's hurry up and get to something meaningful to my life.* Charts and graphs could bore me, especially if I do not associate modern-day relevance with seemingly deep theological rhetoric. I had never studied the tabernacle, although I had heard the subject taught many times and had read the passage each time I read through the Bible.

But when I began to study this passage as part of my research on the table principle, I noticed something interesting about the design of this table. I have a background in interior design; in fact, I owned my own interior design business for about ten years. As designers, there are a few measurements we memorize, and one of them is the average height of a dining table. We often have to purchase fabric to make table skirts, tablecloths, and runners, so it's convenient to know this detail. As I read this passage in Exodus 25, here's what I noticed: the height of the table in the tabernacle was the same height as our dining tables today!

Interested and curious, I continued to read:

> *You shall overlay it with pure gold and make a gold border around it. You shall make for it a rim of a handbreadth around it; and you shall make a gold border for the rim around it.* (vv. 24–25)

God instructed Moses to create a border around the table He designed for the tabernacle. Curious, I glanced at our dining table and noticed that it had a rim around it. Then I looked at our coffee table and realized it had a border around it too. In fact, most of the tables in our home—and, I suspect, most of the tables in your home too—have some kind of rim or edge or border. Most craftsmen find it attractive and important to finish a tabletop with a decorative edge.

The table God designed for the tabernacle is starting to look a lot like a dining table, I thought. My excitement was growing as I continued to read:

> *You shall make four gold rings for it and put rings on the four corners which are on its four feet.* (v. 26)

If you ask a group of kindergartners to draw a picture of a table, how will they draw it? With four corners and four legs. That's the original design for a table, the way most of us picture a table in our minds. Now, since the time of the tabernacle, we have modified the design of tables to include round tables and oval tables and pedestal tables. But the design that God gave for the table in the tabernacle is the kind of table we all picture in our heads: it has four corners and four legs.

Remember, this is taking place more than a thousand years before Christ. As far as I can tell, I am not aware of any documentation in recorded history of a table of this size ever being built before God gave this exact description to Moses. And now the table is a central part of most cultures.

Then I read verse 29:

> *You shall make its dishes and its pans and its jars and its bowls with which to pour drink offerings; you shall make them of pure gold.*

I thought that was fascinating, so I went to my parallel Bible and looked up this verse in various translations. Here are some of the words that I found in that verse: *goblets, spoons, plates, cups, ladles,* and *pitchers*—all for the purpose of pouring out offerings. The priest would take the blood from a slain lamb and use these utensils to pour it out as an offering to God. I thought, *These are similar implements that we use on our own meal tables!*

Thinking back to the drawings and charts of the tabernacle I had seen before, I didn't remember seeing a table set with dishes. So I looked in a few research books at various illustrations of the table in the tabernacle. On most of these drawings, the table did not have plates or dishes or goblets or spoons or pitchers. One illustration sketched a pitcher next to a platter with some pita-like bread stacked on it. But according to God's design as revealed in Exodus 25:29, the table in the tabernacle was set with plates and dishes and pitchers and goblets and spoons!

Curious, I continued reading and discovered God's purpose for the table:

> *You shall set the bread of the Presence on the table before Me at all times.* (v. 30)

Who is the Bread of the Presence? Jesus! Jesus said, "I am the bread of life" (John 6:25, 48). The meal God designed to be set on the table of showbread represented Jesus Himself, the Bread of Life that nourishes us and brings redemption. The Bread of the Presence on the table in the tabernacle was a picture of Jesus, who dwelled as the centerpiece of that table and was the "meal" to be partaken of. The blood of the sacrificed lamb brought redemption for the sins of that day and that year, and it represented the blood of the Lamb who would redeem the sins of everyone for all time. Just imagine Jesus' supernatural, redemptive presence infused the lives of those who brought a sacrifice and allowed the priest to come to the table on their behalf.

Who is the Bread of the Presence? Jesus!

Now, I want you to picture this. In the tabernacle, the ark of the covenant, the dwelling place of the presence of God, was placed behind a very thick, heavy veil. Then the table was placed just outside the veil, on the north side of the tabernacle. God said to Moses, "Put before Me on that table the bread of the Presence—the Presence that will bring redemption." The priests who ministered daily in the tabernacle couldn't see the ark of the covenant with the glory that hovered above it, because it was hidden behind the veil. But they could see the table that was set with the bread of the Presence.

Now, think with me. What happened to the veil in the temple hundreds of years later, after Jesus died? In AD 33, the temple in Jerusalem was a stunning, ornate structure with the same components fashioned from the tabernacle. Rather than being a tent, the temple was a grand edifice. The furnishings, the ark of the covenant, the table, the seven-armed lampstand, and the brass altar were all replicated in the temple from the tabernacle model. When Jesus said, "It is finished!" and breathed His last breath, the thick veil in the temple split in two from top to bottom (Matt. 27:51; Luke 23:45). The presence of God was now exposed; the holiness of God in the ark of the covenant was now open to the redemptive presence of Jesus at the table. What happened when the holiness of God met the redemptive power of the Bread of the Presence? An earthquake! It was a cataclysmic event. Nothing that previously existed remains the same when an earthquake strikes a region. Similarly, when God the Father, the Creator of all of life, is made known and Jesus releases His redemptive presence in our hearts, nothing in our lives remains the same. We experience a life-changing transformation as the Holy Spirit infuses His power in us!

As we will discover in more detail, God meets us with a supernatural presence at the table. This presence of God at the table goes beyond what we do or say, no matter who we are or what we've done. The Bible tells us that God works by grace through faith (Eph. 2:29), and coming to the table is a step of faith, believing that God will meet us there. When we do our part and come to the table, whether we are with our family and friends or alone, the Bread of the Presence meets us there and works in our hearts. Our hearts are formed and shaped with His love and peace as we embrace one another—a fusion of relationships transpires.

> God meets us with a supernatural presence at the table; it is a presence beyond what we do or say, no matter who we are or what we've done.

The Table Principle

The table principle is like a golden thread woven through the tapestry of Scripture, bringing continuity and brilliance and insight. As I studied and prayed, I asked God, "If there is merit in this principle, why haven't I heard this taught in our churches before?" I'm very cautious in how I handle the Word of God, so I wanted to make sure that what I was learning about the table was indeed God's truth.

I've come to understand that the table principle has always been in God's Word, but now is the time we need to hear it, more than ever before. I believe the table principle is God's message to our generation, to strengthen our families and prepare us to do His work in the world today. Previous generations instinctively practiced the table principle and enjoyed the results: lasting relationships, emotional security, and personal motivation. But in contemporary society, our lives are increasingly fragmented by activities and lifestyles and a loss of absolutes that keep us from the family table, and as a result, we are seeing and experiencing the damaging effects in our marriages and families.

> The table principle is a message God is giving to our generation, to strengthen our families and prepare us to do His work in the world today.

As I sat in my chair that day and studied the table God designed for the tabernacle, I thought, *Wait a minute. This table looked like a dinner table. It had dishes, plates, spoons, bowls, and jars—just like our own tables. It was the same height as the dining tables in our homes. It had four corners and four legs, just like many of our tables. And the table was set with the Bread of the Presence...which means that His Presence must also meet us at our own tables!*

Of course, the table of the Bread of the Presence in the tabernacle was not a dining table. The priests did not gather around the table and eat dinner together. Don't misunderstand that. What God is giving here is a principle, not an instruction. Let me pause here and clarify the difference.

An instruction tells you step-by-step how to do something. It is specific to a particular task and is not transferable to other parts of your life. For example, you cannot use instructions on how to bake a cake to instruct you on how to download software. When you follow instructions to complete a task, you do not have to understand the reasoning behind them; you just do exactly what they tell you to do, and you will get the desired result.

A principle, however, is a truth that allows you to use reason. This reasoning leads you to a number of ways that you can apply the principle. Therefore, a principle can be applied to many areas of your life. An example of a biblical principle is whatever you sow, you will reap (Gal. 6:7). Although that is a farming term, this verse is not instructing us about how to plant; it is a principle illustrating that what you plant is what will grow.

So, applying this understanding to the table principle, we see that God is not giving us specific instructions about how to construct tables in our own homes. You do not have to build a table out of acacia wood, twenty-seven inches high, and set gold dishes on the table. And if your dining table happens to be an oval or pedestal, you do not have to get rid of it and buy a table with four corners and four legs. But what we will continue to learn as we search the Scripture and learn the table principle is this: God's original design for the table had the *impression* of the dining tables that you and I use in our own homes. And as we apply the table principle, we will nourish our bodies and our spirits at the table with the redemptive presence of Christ.

As we apply the table principle, we will
nourish our bodies and our spirits at the table
with the redemptive presence of Christ.

An Overview of the Table Principle in Scripture

God's principle of His healing, nourishing, redemptive presence meeting us in a supernatural way as we gather around the table is consistently woven throughout Scripture. Here are brief summaries of a few of the many biblical passages that reveal the table principle and its significance in our lives.

Passover

In the Old Testament, God appointed seven annual celebrations that were set apart as "sacred assemblies" to worship God, to remember what He had done, and to look forward to the redemption He would someday provide (Lev. 23:4 NIV). All the generations of Israelites, including many Jews today, have celebrated these seven annual feasts ever since they were designed by God thousands of years ago. Although each of these feasts involves a significant food or sharing meals in some way, perhaps the most notable example of the table principle is evident in the first celebration, Passover, which takes place during the first month of the Jewish year (Ex. 12:1).

The feast of Passover is a yearly reminder of God's miraculous deliverance of His people from slavery in Egypt. During this feast, Israelites remember God's deliverance by reenacting that awesome event in a family dinner designed as a continuing memorial of His faithfulness to the nation of Israel (Ex. 12:14–17).

One of the most important ordinances of Passover is the Passover meal, called the seder, during which the older generation tells the younger generation the story of the Exodus and explains to them the symbols of the Passover meal: "When your children ask you, 'What does this ceremony mean to you?' then tell them, 'It is the Passover sacrifice to the LORD, who passed over the houses of the Israelites in Egypt and spared our homes when He struck down the Egyptians.'...Because the LORD kept vigil at night to bring them out of Egypt, on this night all the Israelites are to keep vigil to honor the LORD for the generations to come" (Ex. 12:26-27, 42 NIV).

It is significant to point out that the remembrance of the Passover took place *at the table*. The seder is the central part of the Passover celebration, fulfilling the biblical command to retell the Passover story and providing a significant occasion for Jewish families to join together around the table to honor God. Jewish and Christian families who choose to remember these feasts by preparing celebrative meals and retelling stories know that enforcing positive memories from the past builds faith for the future.

Interactions of Jesus

In the New Testament, we see Jesus Christ living out God's design for the table in His daily interactions and teachings. Many of the teachings He imparted to His disciples took place at the table. As one religious scholar notes, "The Gospel of Luke tells about ten milestones in the life of Christ, and each one takes place at a meal."[4] In fact, Jesus was so ready to share a meal with people that the Pharisees and the scribes grumbled, "This man receives sinners and eats with them" (Luke 15:2).

Throughout His public earthly ministry, we see many examples of Jesus sharing meals with people who were considered sinners and outcasts from society, such as Zaccheus the tax collector (Luke 19:5) and Simon the leper (Mark 14:3). To our knowledge, Jesus never turned down a dinner invitation, whether from outcasts or esteemed religious scholars (Luke 7:36).

One of the many examples of Jesus dining with others was when Jesus visited the home of Lazarus, six days before Passover (John 12:1–8). While at the table, Mary expressed her love for Jesus by washing His feet with expensive perfume. In those days, the only way to get to your destination was to walk. If you were prosperous, you might have a donkey. But the primary mode of transportation was your own feet, and they got very tired, hot, dirty, and stinky! Polite hosts would offer cool water for visitors to wash their feet. But for a host to actually wash a weary traveler's feet himself was a very rare and special service indeed.

Imagine the scene: Lazarus, not long before, had been dead and in his tomb for four days before Jesus had miraculously restored him to life. Lazarus's sister Martha was in the kitchen cooking a sumptuous meal. Jesus and His disciples arrived from a hot, dusty journey from the hills of Ephraim. Jesus knew that He would be journeying to the cross in just six days. He dearly wanted to spend some close, warm time with His best friends and disciples. Where does He do this? At the table in their home.

Jesus knew this would be His last opportunity to spend time with His friends Mary, Martha, and Lazarus before His crucifixion. But He didn't choose His final day with them to be among the crowds in the marketplace. He didn't say, "Hey, let's go fishing." No, they gathered at the table. Jesus enjoyed being surrounded by His friends, disciples, and loved ones at the table, where He encouraged them with His presence and modeled truth, instruction, gratitude, serving, and forgiveness.

Jesus enjoyed being surrounded by His friends, disciples, and loved ones at the table.

The Last Supper

The evening before His crucifixion, the final thing Jesus chose to do with the men in whom He had invested His life for three years was to share a meal together—the Passover meal. As we have seen, the seder was a significant meal designed to celebrate God's presence and power, but it was also important to Jesus' purpose at the Last Supper.

The room was borrowed from a wealthy man. We don't know for sure what it looked like, but we know it probably didn't look the way Leonardo da Vinci painted it! When evening came, the meal was prepared and the table was set for Jesus and His twelve disciples.

It is significant to note that none of the disciples was excluded from the Last Supper. During their final meal together before His crucifixion, Jesus shared His table with all twelve of His disciples, including the man He knew would soon betray Him and the one who would vigorously deny Him. At the table, Jesus offered each of His followers grace and companionship, serving them and sharing His presence with them at this Passover meal.

Post-Resurrection Appearances

After Jesus rose from the dead and before He ascended into heaven, He was walking along the road to Emmaus and met Cleopas and his friend. These followers of Jesus were deeply grieved over His crucifixion just days earlier, and in their deep sorrow, they did not recognize Him. Jesus walked with them for a while, and "Beginning with Moses and all the prophets, He explained to them what was said in all the Scriptures concerning Himself" (Luke 24:17).

Yet, after all that walking and talking, Cleopas and his friend still failed to recognize Jesus. It wasn't until they invited Jesus to come in and share a meal with them—when they were breaking bread together *at the table*—that they finally realized that Messiah Himself was in their very midst. "When He was at the table with them, He took bread, gave thanks, broke it and began to give it to them. Then their eyes were opened and they recognized Him" (vv. 30–31).

It was at the table that Cleopas and his friend experienced a supernatural encounter with Christ, the Bread of the Presence, who had been with them all along. This was actually the first "communion" after the death and resurrection of Jesus. Keep in mind that communion was not a religious ritual as we have made it today, but it was communing, or communicating, at a meal together, remembering what Jesus did for them while He was with them. Communion in the New Testament was a table experience.

> Communion in the New Testament was a table experience.

Marriage Supper of the Lamb

The table principle as revealed in Scripture does not stop here on earth. Revelation 19:9 says, "Blessed are those who are invited to the wedding supper of the Lamb."

What is God doing right now? He is setting us a place at the table where He has prepared the marriage supper of the Lamb. The first thing we will do when we enter His presence is to dine together with our bridegroom, Jesus, on our wedding feast.

The Bible tells us that our relationship with Christ is like a bride to her bridegroom (Rev. 21:2, 9). When we create a private, safe place for intimacy with the Lord, we can tell Him everything we think and feel, even if we know that we should not feel that way. It is okay with Him—He's actually not surprised because He knows our hearts anyway! We can verbally express our love for Him and feel His love for us. And we can also give physical expressions of love to our Bridegroom by kneeling or bowing before Him. While they would not all be appropriate for a public worship service, in private intimacy we do not need to feel restricted by how we express our devotion to God.

After living with this kind of intimacy and devotion with my Bridegroom for many years here on earth, my mind can hardly conceive what it will be like to see Him face-to-face one day. The closest thing I can relate my emotions with are the deep butterflies I feel when Larry and I have been apart for several weeks and I see him from a distance as I walk toward him down the airport corridor.

And to think, not only is Jesus waiting for me, but He has prepared an elaborate dinner party for me! As the bride of Christ, you and I will be seated at His table for the wedding feast. In the kingdom of God, we will celebrate our forever intimacy with Christ as we gather at His table, and there is a place reserved for you and for me! Nothing could be more intimate and personal than to see our names written on our place cards at His table in His presence.

From the table in the tabernacle to the marriage supper of the Lamb, God's Word is filled with examples of His intimate, healing, nourishing, and life-changing presence at the table. So let's prepare for a supernatural encounter with God and set our tables!

Table Reflections

1. Like the small leak in the upstairs bathroom, are there ways in which you've been overlooking your family table, not thinking of the long-term consequences?

2. State how you plan to "repair your leak" by creating a new positive habit of coming together at the table regularly in your home.

3. Who is the Bread of the Presence?

4. What was the purpose of the table in the tabernacle?

5. List three events where Jesus sat at the table with others. What was the significance of these dinners?

Chapter 3

Setting Your Table

She has prepared her food, she has mixed her wine; She has also set her table.

—Proverbs 9:2

I HAVE THE MOST MARVELOUS ring on my finger, filled with dazzling stones. But it wasn't always that way. My wedding ring is a combination of the broken and the undiscovered.

Several years ago, when Larry and I were approaching our fortieth wedding anniversary, he wanted to give me a meaningful anniversary present. But we had no steady income, because Larry had recently left the pastorate to pursue the vision for a new ministry that by faith we were birthing. One day, he looked at my wedding ring and said, "Devi, more than anything, I would love to replace that pathetic ring on your hand."

"Don't worry about it, honey," I said. "This isn't the time. We've put everything we have into what we believe God has called us to do now. Replacing my wedding ring is the least on my list."

But then I remembered something. I told Larry, "I have an idea. There is a little box that your mother left in her things ten years ago. And in that box, there are a lot of broken pieces of jewelry, including a watch she gave me that has about two carats of small diamonds in it. There are a couple of old tennis bracelets with little tiny chipped diamonds, and I have a few pieces of broken jewelry in there too. Why don't you take everything in that box to the jeweler and see what he can do with it? That way we aren't spending any money, but putting together those broken pieces would make a beautiful ring for me." Larry knows that I like wide bands with pavé settings, that's lots of tiny stones put together, so he agreed to do that.

Larry took the box filled with fragmented, broken pieces to the jeweler. None of the jewels had value in themselves. These tiny, chipped pieces couldn't be worn, they couldn't be used, and they couldn't be repaired. They had been treated as insignificant and sat in a box, unused, for more than ten years.

A few days after Larry took the box to the jeweler, I got a phone call. "I've made a discovery," the jeweler told me. "When I lifted up the cotton lining of the box, I found a stone wrapped in wax paper. It's a marquis. Do you want me to work this into your ring?"

I said, "Why not?" I didn't know what this stone looked like; I didn't even know it was there. I just thought Larry's mom, coming from the Depression mentality, somehow got this stone and then she hid it under the lining of her jewelry box. Larry and I did not know we had this stone, even though it had been in our house for a decade.

When the ring was finished, I was amazed at how beautiful it was. I couldn't believe how all those broken and chipped pieces could become something so stunning and valuable! That's exactly what happens when you bring together the broken and the undiscovered—you receive unexpected blessings.

Your home may feel fragmented, with everyone going different directions every night of the week, pursuing many interests. As long as all the pieces of your family remain apart, they have no sense of value. But when you bring together the broken and the fragmented parts of your family, around the table, and discover each one's unique gifts, you will experience a dazzling restoration of value worth more than you could ever dream. Each person's potential begins to be revealed.

The Dignity and Sanctity of the Home

Throughout Scripture, we see that God has conferred dignity and sanctity on the institution of the home. God established the first family in the garden of Eden, and He gave Adam and Eve clear instructions about His design for marriage and family. I think it is significant that God set the family in order *before* giving the Law and before sending His Son to the cross. God even chose the marriage relationship to portray our relationship with Him.

The home is where our hearts are formed. No matter how much we may try to base our lives on something else—such as sports, education, national security, economics, or even the church—we cannot change the reality that all of the physical, emotional, and spiritual development in the human soul starts at home.

The home is where our hearts are formed.

However, in our society, the home has often ceased to be the center of family activity. Instead of spending time together in the evenings, gathered around the table to share stories and relate with one another, moms and dads and children are frequently splintered in different directions—work, daycare centers, baseball diamonds, football fields, dance studios, gymnasiums, civic centers, and so on. Even excessive church activities usurp the time a family needs at home. We are so busy shuttling our children to various sports and activities that most of our family dinners come from a fast-food window and are gulped down in the backseat of a car. A recent study by Roper Public Affairs & Media found that 80 percent of Americans feel that it is hard to find the time to eat together regularly.[1]

What happened to the dignity and the sanctity of the home? How did we move so far off course? In this chapter, we will see why the value of the home has slowly eroded, and then we will explore practical ways you can put together the broken pieces of your family to restore the dignity and sanctity of your home by setting your table.

What Happened to the Home?

As Christians, we have an enemy who fears the presence of God. Satan knows that he cannot overpower God, so he seeks instead to undermine God's authority in our lives. And one of Satan's most effective strategies is to keep us so busy that we are no longer at home.

You see, the enemy knows who we are. If we love Jesus and are followers of God, he usually doesn't tempt us to sin overtly. For example, I am very much in love with my husband and committed to our marriage, so the enemy does not tempt me to have a sexual relationship with another man. And I'm not tempted to steal a magazine at the checkout lane of a grocery store or to rob the cashier at gunpoint. No, the enemy doesn't often tempt us with obvious sins like that. As Christians who believe in the power of God and the redemption of Jesus and the empowering presence of the Holy

Spirit, the enemy's most effective plan against us is to tweak us just enough off-center to render us powerless. He distracts us by making sure we are so busy doing good things that we don't have time to come home and set the table.

If home is where our hearts are formed, then the table is where our hearts are connected. At the table, we experience the Bread of the Presence, the redemptive presence of Jesus that strengthens our marriages and unites our families and nourishes our hearts. I think the enemy's goal for us is something like this: *I can't get those who truly know Christ to deny Him, but I can get them to become so busy that they no longer come to the table, where the redemptive presence of Jesus dwells.*

> If home is where our hearts are formed, then the table is where our hearts are connected.

When I was growing up, there was a difference between the life-styles of Christian families and non-Christian families. My family was involved in church-related activities that non-Christian families did not do, and we did not participate in all the activities other families did. But these days, church-attending families often do everything non-church-attending families do: we have our kids in the same sports, lessons, and community programs of every kind. Many of us take each of our kids to a different activity every day of the week. And then, on top of all that activity and involvement, we add church. So in addition to all their sports and extracurricular activities, our children also attend midweek youth group meetings, praise team practice, and church service, while we participate in an adult Bible study, volunteer in several ministries, and go to leadership training. As I have observed Christian families in our church and across the nation, I have come to believe that the reason the divorce rate is higher among churchgoing families is because we are at home less!

Let me be clear that each of these activities is a good thing by itself. There is nothing inherently wrong with sports or lessons or community involvement or church participation. In fact, some of these are even essential. However, not a single one or even all of these activities put together can replace the nurturing environment of a healthy home. Who we become is a direct reflection of where we spend our time.

> Who we become is a direct reflection of where we spend our time.

Larry and I began to notice this trend toward overcommitment several years ago, while we were still pastoring a church. We observed well-intentioned Christian families who, out of a healthy desire to become involved and to help, agreed to serve or lead in several different ministries of the church. As a result, these men and women, fathers and mothers, were often at church several nights of the week, serving in multiple ministries. But back home, no one was at the table! So Larry made an important decision to help these families: our church began to limit each person's involvement to one area of ministry. Pick a ministry, we told them, and do it with all your heart. Be fully involved in that area, but then the other nights of the week, go home and gather around your table with your family! In this way, our church helped families set healthy boundaries and restore the importance of the family table in their homes.

The dinner table is the only place where a family sits forty-two inches apart, face to face, and talks for thirty minutes to an hour. The table is the place where our souls are nourished and our character is formed. And it is the place where the supernatural presence of God Himself comes to us and works in our hearts.

Has your life become so busy that you are no longer coming to your table? Whether you are married or single, with or without children, the Bread of the Presence wants to meet with you at your family table. He is knocking at your door, inviting you to come and dine with Him, but are you too distracted to hear Him? If so, then you are missing out on the incredible spiritual renewing of His Presence at your table.

> Has your life become so busy that you are no longer coming to your table?

Perhaps your family has valuable gifts that haven't been discovered and put to use, because you've been broken or split apart. You're busy doing God's work, doing good things, serving and helping. But Jesus' invitation to us is, "Behold, I stand at the door and knock; if anyone hears My voice and opens the door, *I will come in to him and will dine with him, and he with Me*" (Rev. 3:20; emphasis added). Jesus wants to come in and sit at your table. But for Him to come and dine with us, we must first set our table.

Important Questions to Answer

1. Out of twenty-one regular meals each week, how many does your family eat together, on average?

2. What barriers are preventing you from increasing that number?

3. What could you do to remove some of those barriers and increase the number of meals your family eats together?

A Wise Woman Sets Her Table

The book of Proverbs reveals to us God's design of the way of wisdom. Proverbs 9:2 says, "She has prepared her food, she has mixed her wine. She has also set *her table*" (emphasis added). Who is "she" in this verse? Wisdom! Here is the principle we learn: it is wisdom for us to prepare what we are having for dinner and to set our table. It is important for us to plan ahead and think about what our family is going to have for dinner.

> It is wisdom for us to prepare what we are having for dinner and to set our table.

You may think that your schedule is too busy for you to prepare your table. After all, you and your kids are participating in activities almost every weeknight and weekend! Perhaps you think you don't have time to go to the grocery store or local delicatessen to buy the food necessary for a nutritious family meal. I realize that you are busy, and I know that this is going to take some effort and creative thinking on your part. But if we want to experience the Bread of the Presence, the redemptive presence of Jesus that meets us in our homes, we must find a way to come home and to set our table.

I secured a professional videographer to film promotional footage for this book. When he arrived, his wife was his assistant. I was excited to meet her and immediately engaged in conversation that revealed she and her husband had been married for three years and together were blending a family of six children.

We began filming, and she heard me talk passionately about the message of this book. Afterward, she made a few defensive comments about the hectic nature of their family dinners. I wanted to take her home with me and love her, listen to her heart, and gently guide her.

I wanted to build her confidence and elevate her value in relationship to her family and new husband. But they packed their equipment, and we said good-bye.

The next morning, the local church sanctuary was crowded. When I stood to speak, I looked to my left and sitting on the third row was this family: Dad, Mom, and six lovely children with ages ranging from elementary to late teens. After I spoke on the table principle, I asked families to stand to acknowledge that they want to do better in bringing their families to a table experience. Their family stood, along with many of the families in the sanctuary. I prayed for the standing families and concluded my message.

At the autograph table following the service, the wife came up to me and said, "You rocked my world! I will never be the same after hearing the message."

It takes time for the divisions of families to heal, and this loving mother made a commitment that morning to allow her world to be "rocked," turned upside down. She left that church service determined to bring all their children around the table to experience the Bread of the Presence that can heal their hearts and unite their blended family.

Keepers of the Home

Titus 2:5 tells us that women are the keepers of the home. This, of course, does not mean that women are slaves to their home, nor does it mean that women have to stay at home all day, every day. The idea of being a "keeper" of your home means that you have been entrusted by God with the responsibility of overseeing your household, to keep it running well and honoring God. Professional or personal pursuits do not change the fact that God designed women to be the primary influencers in the home.

The idea of being a "keeper" of your home
means that you have been entrusted by
God with the responsibility of overseeing
your household, to keep it running well and
honoring God.

Right now, women have more public influence and achievements than ever before, and yet we seem to be more dissatisfied than ever. Why is this? I believe it is because no matter what you have achieved or how esteemed you are in your professional world, if your children are rebelling and your home is filled with strife and chaos, you are not going to be fulfilled. But you don't have to trade fruitfulness and work outside the home. They can go hand in hand. You simply have to make sure that you are "keeping" your home, so that even when you are away, you do the things that are necessary to make sure your home is orderly and peaceful and God-honoring.

Regardless of whether or not you also work outside the home, let's face it: the woman is the scheduler of the family. You are the one who signs up your children for school activities and Little League, and you are the one who shuttles your kids to and from soccer practice and dance lessons and birthday parties. And so it is up to you, the keeper of your home, to make the table experience a priority in your family life. What is on your calendar for tomorrow? Think through what your day will look like, and then come up with a plan: *This is what I need to prepare dinner.* This is the way of wisdom. It's not wisdom to drive through a fast-food restaurant at the last minute!

My daughter-in-law, Kim, has two young daughters and also works outside the home as an assistant professor of mathematics at High Point University in North Carolina. In chapter 5, she shares practical tips on how she is able to prepare simple, nutritious meals for her family while managing a full-time outside job.

My friend Marilyn, who worked as a high school teacher while her children were at home, is living proof that it is possible to work full-time, raise a family, enjoy married life, and still serve meals regularly at the table. What was Marilyn's secret? She was willing to pay the price—to do whatever it took to allow time for her family meals. She accomplished this by learning to pray, prioritize, and plan. She said, "I wanted my children to someday look back with fond memories of our time and meals together. I decided when my children were young what 'Mom's home cooking' would look like. I wanted them to remember their mealtimes as being fun, relational, delicious, and nutritious. Now that my children are grown and in college, I can assure you that I would once again make eating meals together at the table a priority."

When my children were young, preparing a meal required making everything from scratch. But today's grocery store aisles are filled with prepared foods to help you put a nutritious meal on the table. You can buy trays of assorted fresh vegetables and individually frozen servings of fruit. And you can even buy fresh-baked bread and tortillas! When we set aside a few minutes each day to plan our meals, we can more easily follow the way of wisdom by picking up fresh, healthy foods from the store or the local deli to create nutritious meals for our family.

Fun Family Centerpiece Ideas

Boys' night: Use a dump truck to hold a potted plant.

Girls' night: Use a jewelry box to hold a small potted plant. Add cascading beads.

Dad's night: Sports caps or helmets can hold a potted plant. Goblets can become pedestals holding baseballs or tennis balls.

Mom's night: Fresh flowers and candlelight always make Mom feel special.

What if your husband doesn't get home from work until late? You may be tempted to feed the kids and leave the leftovers in the refrigerator for your husband to heat up when he gets home. But don't deprive your husband of the Bread of the Presence! And please don't create for your children a life apart from their father. If your husband works late, I suggest you give your kids a snack, give them their bath, put them in their pajamas, and read them a bedtime story...and then when your husband gets home, you and the children eat with him, as a family—even if it's just sharing dessert together. If your husband does shift work and is gone all night, your family meal could be breakfast or even lunch. It's not important which meal you choose to eat together as your regular family meal; the important thing is that you are spending time with one another around your table. There are many creative solutions for parents who work late hours or shift work. Discuss this with your spouse and find a way for your family to eat together at your table regularly.

Make Your Table a Place of Pleasure

One way you can make your table a place of pleasure is by using nice dishes, placemats, and a tablecloth. I suggest that you sometimes use your china or very best dishes for your family, so they feel just as important as any special guest. By making a few small efforts to set the stage and prepare the meal, you are conferring dignity and honor on your family members.

When you are setting your table, it doesn't have to be elaborate. You don't have to use expensive place settings or create a centerpiece from fresh flowers grown in your own garden. When you use what you have, with a little forethought and a lot of love, you can make a beautiful table!

When you use what you have, with a little forethought and a lot of love, you can make a beautiful table!

When I unload my dishwasher, I always put my plates directly back onto my table, instead of across the entire kitchen back into the cabinets where I keep them. In my house, the table is much closer to the dishwasher anyway! Keeping your table set with pretty place settings, as I do in my home, can be a way of welcoming people into your home and into your life. Now, this doesn't mean your table has to look like a display in a department store—so beautiful that no one actually eats on it! But we can all use what we have to set our table and make our table warm and inviting.

Setting the table is not only an act of wisdom, but it is an act of service to your family. Let's face it: there will likely be many evenings when you may not want to fix dinner or prepare the table for your children and husband. And sometimes, it will be necessary to drive through or pick up dinner on your way home. But when you make family meals a priority in your home, you are choosing to honor God and to

Creative Table Covers

- Use a quilt when serving a home-cooked country menu.

- New colorful bed sheets in all kinds of prints and patterns can create various table themes.

- Black fabric is a great background for placemats and table squares. Add animal print, such as zebra and leopard!

- Linen or terry dishtowels serve well as placemats. Lay them on the table so the length creates the drop over the table.

- Colorful chargers served under the dinner plate give variety and saves the tablecloth from spills.

- Shimmering fabrics are great to use under chargers for the holidays.

- Lace curtains from a secondhand store work well as an over-lay for a Victorian tea theme.

Enhance the Table Experience for the Entire Family . . .

- Play music while eating at your table.

- At times, use your best dishes for your family, not only for guests.

- Meals should be prepared for the liking of the adults. However, always provide an item that you know your children love.

- For quick casual meals, use colorful paper plates and napkins, and light a candle.

invite His presence into your home, giving Him the opportunity to work in your family's hearts and lives.

You can also involve your children in preparing the meal, teaching them by example how to serve. By choosing to set the table in our homes, we are training our children, the next generation, by showing them in tangible ways how to serve their future families by setting the tables in their own homes.

Make the Table a Priority

Since feminism emerged in the 1950s and '60s, our homes have been redesigned with bars and counters in the kitchen, instead of setting aside a place for the table. When I consider how many homes do not have adequate space for a kitchen table, I think the enemy of our souls might be saying, *I know what I'll do! If I can get families to sit side by side, facing a wall when they eat, then they'll emotionally disconnect. They'll be so busy that they will eventually stop eating together.* After all, when we are emotionally disconnected, we no longer see a need to eat together at the same time. And soon, we no longer gather at the table.

As I teach the table principle in conferences all across the country, I am often approached by women who say, "Devi, we don't even have a table in our home." Don't let that be an obstacle that keeps you from obeying God by setting your table! I encourage you to go out and buy an inexpensive table this week. Or use a card table. Or put a plank on top of a couple of sawhorses and cover it with a table-cloth. You can make a table. It doesn't have to be beautiful or fancy; it just needs to be a useable place where your family can gather, face-to-face, and enjoy the Bread of the Presence together.

Another question I am often asked is, "Devi, what about my husband? He won't sit at the table anymore. He just wants to eat in front of the TV." If your husband refuses to come to the table, then I have a suggestion: get a TV tray, and then lovingly set a place on that tray for your husband. Put a cloth on it and then make his plate. As you prepare his table, pray over it, saying, "Lord, do your work in my husband's heart." Then take the table to him and sit beside him on the couch as he eats his dinner. If you have children, you and the children can eat together at the table while your husband eats his meal at his own tray. If you continue to honor him and set his table, hopefully he will be joining you and the children at the table, where the supernatural Bread of the Presence will transform his heart and unite your family.

In this hectic world, mealtimes may be the only opportunity for your family to share precious time together. If you want to set your table, you have to make it a high priority. Review your family's schedule, and find a way to make it possible to eat dinner together. As family expert Becky Hein says, "Even if it's one or two dinners a week, with the TV off, that's better than none at all."2

> In this hectic world, mealtimes may be the only opportunity for your family to share precious time together.

Are you willing to try something you may have never done before? Will you commit to make it a priority to gather together at the table with your family members on a regular basis? At first, it won't be easy. Dads will have to commit to coming home from work earlier or to arranging another mealtime to spend together with the family. Moms will need to prepare menus in advance. Children should help set the table and help clear it after dinner. Everyone should do the dishes together. The objective is for the entire family to join together with purpose.

If families all across America would once again come to the table, can you imagine how much stronger and healthier our families would be? Let's set the table and bring the scattered and fragmented families back to the table, where Jesus promises that He will dine with you and transform your lives with His redemptive presence.

Wives, husbands, singles, I call on you to make a new commitment—one that will bring the power of redemption to your family in a more significant, supernatural way than you've ever experienced it before. Don't let the enemy continue to distract your family and keep you away from the table. Instead, make a commitment to God and to one another that you will gather daily around your family table, and then live with the confident assurance that God's presence is with you every day as you grow together in God's grace and power.

Table Reflections

1. Complete this sentence: If home is where the heart is _____, then the table is where the heart is _____.

2. What busy activities are on your calendar that keep you from setting your table?

3. What items do you need to collect to improve the appearance of your table?

4. What biblical virtue in Proverbs 9:2 is identified with those who set their table?

5. List the steps you can take to make preparing for meals and setting your table a priority.

Chapter 4
Seats of Honor

"Don't be afraid," David said to him, "for I will surely show you kindness... and you will always eat at my table."
—2 Samuel 9:7 NIV

S EVERAL YEARS AGO, I met a beautiful Dominican woman named Cecelia. She had been delivered from a lifestyle of immorality and was a wonderful, committed believer in Jesus Christ. When Cecelia heard about the Mentoring Mansion, she volunteered to serve there. She had heard that we offered the ladies foot massages during their stay at the mansion, so she volunteered to do the foot rubs and to embellish their toenails with nail art.

Now don't get me wrong on this: I think it is a great service to give foot rubs. I myself give foot massages to the ladies at the Mentoring Mansion on a regular basis. But in this circumstance, when Cecelia volunteered to serve the ladies at the mansion in this way, the Holy Spirit impressed me as if to say, *She can do so much more than rub feet.*

I was curious to find out what God had in store for this precious lady, and I wanted to get to know her better. So I invited her to my house for a cup of tea.

"No, Devi," she responded, kindly but firmly. "I cannot come to your house."

I assumed she must have been busy on the day I suggested. So I said, "That's okay, Cece," as I affectionately called her. "We'll find a better time. When can you come over, then?" I was trying to think of how we could rearrange our schedules to find a time when she was available.

"No, no," she insisted, her gaze drifting down to her feet. "I *can't* come to your house."

At that moment, I realized what was going on—she didn't feel worthy of coming to my house and eating at my table. I assured her, "Cecelia, I am inviting you to my home as my honored guest, and I really want you to come."

She reluctantly agreed, and we set the date.

When Cecelia arrived, we sat at my small drop-leaf table in the corner of my kitchen. I lit a small candle and had picked some flowers from my yard. The table was too worn to be exposed, so I had covered the scarred tabletop with a white cloth embroidered with small pastel flowers. The tea was served from a delicate patterned teapot and poured into china cups with matching saucers. On the side of the saucer were demi spoons I had brought from Germany many years ago. I had not prepared a fancy tea complete with scones and sandwiches—I didn't have time that day for such a thing. We simply had a cup of tea in my kitchen and enjoyed insightful conversation for one hour. Cecelia was overwhelmed with the presentation of the table, although to me it was very simple.

"I can't believe you did this for me," she said. She then shared her story with me. Social programs had not given Cece confidence and self-value, but her encounter with Jesus had transformed her life. Her drug-addicted years of despair had been replaced with a life of purpose and meaning. However, she had a difficult time talking to me without apologizing and considering herself unworthy to be in my home. Shame still had a grip on her self-esteem. I explained to her the reason that I wanted this time with her. Although I was grateful that she came to assist at the Mentoring Mansion with bedtime foot massages, I wanted to discover her other gifts. I knew there was more.

Cecelia had convinced herself that because of the things she had done in her past, she was not worthy of being anyone's invited guest. But that day, I elevated her and restored her dignity by giving her a place of honor at my table. At my table that day, she discovered gifts and talents that had been bottled up but not yet released. Cecelia was smart, creative, and very entrepreneurial. After sipping a simple cup of tea at a table especially prepared for her, she was encouraged to begin setting her own table for her children. And before long, she started a small business and shared hope with others. Inviting her to share a cup of tea at my table communicated my love for her and helped her gradually become a radiant, grateful woman.

There's something very powerful about the table. When somebody feels unwanted, rejected, and less than valuable, you can bring them to your table and their sense of personal value will be elevated. Could it be that's why Jesus said, "I tell you the truth, anyone who gives you a cup of water in my name because you belong to Christ will certainly not lose his reward" (Matt 9:41 NIV)?

> When somebody feels unwanted, rejected, and
> less than valuable, you can bring them to your
> table and their sense of personal value will be
> elevated.

As we saw in chapter 2, God gives us many instructions and illustrations in the Bible about the importance of the dinner experience in our homes and our families, as a place where His supernatural presence meets with us. In the Old Testament, we are given a beautiful example of how a rejected, fearful man's dignity and position were restored when he was given a seat of honor at the king's table.

A Place at the King's Table

In the nation of Israel, about one thousand years before Christ, a young boy was born into royalty and privilege; he was the son of Jonathan and the grandson of King Saul, the first king of Israel. For the first few years of his life, this young prince lived in peace and, as far as we know, had a happy childhood. But outside of his idyllic home life, national events were taking a turn for the worse. King Saul was losing his grip on his mind as well as his kingdom. God told Saul that He had chosen David to be of the next king of Israel—instead of Saul's own son, Jonathan. Saul was enraged, and he set out to destroy David and his ragtag army.

Saul's insane fury led to many defeats on the battlefield, including a devastating loss to the Philistines that resulted in the deaths of Saul and three of his sons, including the prince's father, Jonathan. When the boy's nurse heard of Saul's defeat, she grabbed the young prince and fled, knowing that in those brutal days, when a new regime took over, the conquering nation would hunt down and murder every descendant of the previous king, to prevent them from usurping the throne. As the grandson of King Saul and the son of Prince Jonathan, the boy was in immediate danger. The nurse knew she had to act at once to spare the boy's life.

Yet in her well-intentioned haste to save her beloved young charge from certain death, the nurse accidentally dropped the boy, causing both of his feet to be permanently crippled. His life was spared, but it would never be the same.

Some of you may be familiar with this tragic story of young Mephibosheth, recorded for us in 1 Samuel 31. But many years later, this same young man, who had fled his childhood home in fear and was a helpless cripple, living in fear and shame far away from the palace in a desolate place, received a very unexpected and life-altering offer of grace.

In the course of time, David defeated the Philistines and the other enemies of Israel, restoring the throne and expanding the borders of the nation. The Lord gave David victory wherever he went, and he became the most celebrated king in Israel's history.

In 2 Samuel 9, David was enjoying a time of peace and perhaps feeling a bit nostalgic about his friend Jonathan, remembering the covenant they had made with each other many years earlier. Turning to his servant Ziba, David asks, "Is there not yet anyone of the house of Saul to whom I may show the kindness of God?"

> *Ziba said to the king, "There is still a son of Jonathan who is crippled in both feet." So the king said to him, "Where is he?" And Ziba said to the king, "Behold, he is in the house of Machir the son of Ammiel in Lo-debar." Then King David sent and brought him from the house of Machir the son of Ammiel, from Lo-debar. Mephibosheth, the son of Jonathan the son of Saul, came to David and fell on his face and prostrated himself. And David said, "Mephibosheth." And he said, "Here is your servant!" (2 Sam. 9:3–6)*

Just imagine how Mephibosheth must have felt, this man crippled in both feet, raised by a stranger, living far away from the palace that was his rightful home. He likely felt rejected, sad, and lonely. And just as he had feared the Philistines' brutal slaying of all royal heirs, when Mephibosheth heard that King David was looking for him, he surely was terrified that the new king was hunting down and eradicating the last remaining descendants of Saul. The very thing he had feared his entire life was coming true! And what would be the fate of Mephibosheth's wife and young son? Would they be slain as well? He bowed low before the new king and awaited his impending judgment.

> David said to him, "Do not fear, for I will surely show kindness to you for the sake of your father Jonathan, and will restore to you all the land of your grandfather Saul; and **you shall eat at my table regularly**." (2 Sam. 9:7; emphasis added)

What a picture of grace! Instead of destroying the grandson of the former king, David told Mephibosheth, "You'll not only get your inheritance, but you will *also* get to eat at my table!"

In this beautiful passage, David honored his covenant with Jonathan by elevating Mephibosheth and giving him a place at the king's table. David took Jonathan's crippled son, a man who could not serve the king as a warrior or servant and who certainly wasn't deemed worthy of sitting at a king's table. To this man, David said, "I am going to restore your confidence. Come here, son of my best friend, Jonathan. Grandson of King Saul. I'm going to honor you and keep my covenant with your father by giving you an honored place at my table." David restored him and erased his pain of rejection by saying, "You will always eat at my table." By eating regularly at the table of the king, Mephibosheth's personal value and self-esteem were renewed.

Physically challenged and crippled people are often socially ignored. By bringing him to his table, King David let Mephibosheth know that he was as important as everyone else. And thus, Mephibosheth's dignity as the grandson of Israel's first king was restored.

David could have given him a room at the palace or a large amount of money. But all the money in the world couldn't undo his shame and rejection. So David met the greatest need in Mephibosheth's life—his need for acceptance and dignity—by giving him a place of honor at the king's table.[1]

> No matter how fancy or frugal your home may be, there's something special about giving someone a place at your table.

Home-Cooked Hospitality

No matter how fancy or frugal your home may be, there's something special about giving someone a place at your table. Isn't it true that you can meet people in a restaurant, but when you are invited to come into their home, it's much more intimate and honoring? During the forty-plus years that Larry and I have been inviting people into our home to share a meal with us, I have learned that most people prefer to be given an honored place at your table for a simple home-cooked meal rather than to be taken out, even to the finest of restaurants.

In *The Joy of Hospitality*, Vonette Bright recalls learning that lesson the hard way.

> When Dr. Bill Fletcher, a friend from Oklahoma City, came to Los Angeles on business, he called to say that he had a free evening. My [husband] Bill called from his office to tell me

that he had invited Dr. Fletcher to dinner. I said, "Good, we'll take him out."

Bill was silent. "It's Monday," I quickly explained. "I've been doing laundry all day. I'm tired and have nothing to serve but hamburgers."

Bill sighed. "Okay, we'll take him out."

I had forgotten that most of the fine restaurants in Los Angeles were closed on Mondays. We drove to every one we knew, found them all closed, and became more embarrassed as we drove. Finally, we ended up going to Dr. Fletcher's hotel and, at his insistence, were his guests for dinner.

As we ended the evening, Dr. Fletcher thanked us for a lovely time. But I'll never forget his gracious remark as we parted. "For your future information, I would far rather have had [crumbs from your table], Vonette, than to eat at any fancy restaurant in all of Los Angeles."

"The next time you come to town, we'll have you in our home for dinner," I promised.

But there was no next time. Bill Fletcher passed away a few months later. Many times since, I've reminded myself that it does not matter whether my home is fancy or plain, the food elaborate or simple. It is the hospitality that people respond to.[2]

Showing hospitality starts at home. Giving your children a seat of honor at your table is a powerful way to demonstrate that they have a place of privilege in your family. Mealtimes in your home can be so much more than a short break when your children emerge from their bedrooms to grab some chips in the pantry or warm up leftovers. As you begin to understand that God designed the table to be a place of dignity and sanctity in your home, you can start setting your children a place of honor at your table, restoring their self-worth and giving the supernatural Bread of the Presence an opportunity to work in their hearts.

Think about it: what do we do when we are going to celebrate a birthday and want to make our children feel important and special? We set the table! We use a fancy tablecloth and sometimes even give the birthday child a special plate. When our children are young, we might set their birthday table with paper plates and cups of their favorite cartoon character—something they would appreciate and enjoy. On birthdays, we give our children an honored place at the table as a way of expressing our love and affirmation of their worth and dignity.

This is a great tradition. But let's not stop at birthdays! Instead, let's create seats of honor for our spouse and children every time we gather for family meals. No, that doesn't mean you have to use themed place settings for every meal. But you can make the most of what you have. As I mentioned earlier, don't save your nicest dishes only for guests; use them for the ones you love and want to honor the most. Even if you are serving a simple, ordinary meal, you can demonstrate to each member of your family that he or she has a place of honor at your table.

> Let's create seats of honor for our spouse and children every time we gather for family meals.

The Special Glass

My friend Harriet recently shared with me a creative way her family shows honor to one another at their family table.

> To celebrate our fifteenth wedding anniversary, my husband, Bill, and I spent a weekend on Catalina Island. Our time together was delightful as we enjoyed a variety of great restaurants along with some casual sightseeing and, of course, a little bit of shopping here and there.

While at Catalina, we discovered that crystal was the gift designated for the fifteenth wedding anniversary. We desired to find something along our way that would be a sentimental keepsake for years to come. While we were browsing in a nautical-themed gift shop, something caught our eye. It was a goblet with a sailboat etched on the glass. Since our family was fascinated with sailing, this $2.50 glass (obviously, not crystal) seemed to be the perfect find.

During that getaway, Bill and I shared a precious prayer time, asking God to bring us a crystal-like transparency with Him and with each other. We brought the goblet home, and I found a perfect place for it in our hutch along with some delicate, stunning crystal pieces that were wedding gifts. I didn't realize the treasure that glass would become.

It was several months later, when our son, Wil, was celebrating his ninth birthday, that I had the idea of placing the goblet by his plate at the dinner table. That was the beginning of many memories we have enjoyed over the years using "the special glass," as we fondly call it, for family celebrations.

In addition to the birthday celebrations, the special glass has appeared at our children's dinner plates for getting a good grade on a spelling test, playing the violin at a spring recital, scoring a goal in soccer, assisting a soccer goal (which we thought was a higher achievement), as well as showing good sportsmanship. Passing their drivers' tests brought three cheers and the special glass. And yes, Mom and Dad, too, were honored with the special glass on different occasions.

When each of our children was engaged to be married, we placed the special glass at the plate of our newly welcomed family member. It was fun hearing our children, Wil, Stephanie, and Sarah, tell their future mates some of the history and stories surrounding the special glass.

One tender story that comes to mind took place when Stephanie was on her high school volleyball team. It was her senior year, and they had more than enough girls to form the varsity team. The coach asked Stephanie if she would like to play on the junior varsity team, as well as the varsity team, in order to get more playing time. She eagerly accepted the offer, understanding she would practice with both teams: two hours with junior varsity followed by two hours with varsity, totaling a hefty four hours of serving, setting, and spiking! I was amazed at Stephanie's spirit to keep that rigorous schedule. She loved the game, and she loved the teams. Yet after a few games, it was evident that, even with the practice commitment, she played only the last couple of minutes of the varsity games.

My heart broke for her. With irritation, I wondered, *Doesn't the coach see her potential? Her skill? Her heart? Doesn't she see Stephanie's submission to the coach's authority?* It wasn't easy going to those games.

At one of the final tournament varsity games of the season, the coach approached our daughter during the pregame warm-ups and asked her to leave the court, explaining that she was replacing her with a freshman JV player. The coach then told Stephanie to return to the locker room, change clothes, and give the substitute her uniform. The coach's final instruction was, "After you change your uniform, I want you to come back to the gym, sit on the bleachers, and cheer for the team." It was a demoralizing experience, to say the least.

Bill and I rarely missed a game; however, we were out of town for this one. My friend Nancy sat in the bleachers that night, observing the awkward encounter. In my absence, my friend became the surrogate mother Stephanie needed. Nancy followed Stephanie into the locker room and held her while she cried. To this day, I'm exceedingly grateful for Nancy's sensitivity and compassion in that moment.

Later that evening, when Stephanie arrived home, she told us about the incident. Trying to rein in our anger and disappointment, we cried and comforted our child. I'll not forget the short time of prayer we had together kneeling by our bed, asking the Lord to help us, to give us His peace and comfort. After that prayer time, I wondered if Stephanie would quit the team. After all, the season was almost over. Bill asked Stephanie what she wanted to do. She responded immediately, "Well, I'm not quitting, that's for sure!"

The next night, the special glass was beside Stephanie's plate. It was a symbol that celebrated her tenacity, her loyalty to the team, and her perseverance. We didn't mention or draw attention to the special glass. No words were needed, because her appreciative smile said it all.

A few days later, the varsity team, who had witnessed the coach's lack of discretion at the tournament game, pooled their money and gave Stephanie a volleyball along with a card they had designed and signed, which celebrated Stephanie and awarded her the MVP for the season. Indeed, she was!

The special glass is not special because it was expensive, or because it was an heirloom, or a gift from a friend. It's special because in our family, it is a simple way to celebrate and honor the treasures who sit around our table.

Traditions—Keeping Memories Alive

It is never too late to begin a new family tradition, like the special glass Harriet uses in her family. Sometimes, depending on the tradition you start, it can cost you time and money. However, in the long run, beginning new traditions will prove to be worthwhile in keeping family connections alive.

At the Mentoring Mansion, eight ladies come to spend four days with me each month to learn home management and vital relationship skills. Recently, one of my guests was from an aristocratic British family. While we were eating a meal, she shared with us the British tradition of the napkin ring.

When a child is born into a British family, a silver napkin ring is monogrammed and presented to the infant as a gift from the mother and father. When the child is old enough to sit at the table, this napkin ring holds her cloth napkin at each meal. It serves as the place card, marking where to sit, and it also identifies her napkin because the napkin is not necessarily laundered after each meal. When a person is married, the bride's napkin ring goes with her, and the groom's ring comes with him. When they have children, the tradition repeats itself. When a family member dies, his or her napkin ring is passed down to a family member. The tradition of passing the napkin ring passes family memories of the dinner experience from one generation to another.

My guest was overwhelmed with the memories of her family table as she heard me speak about the table principle. She had rebelled against the rigidity of her family's aristocratic lifestyle and had chosen to live her life in a very different way. It was while she was sitting at the table of the Mentoring Mansion that her hardened heart softened. She realized that she had been given a gift, not only the gift of silver napkin rings from generations since the 1700s, but also the gift of the table memories those napkin rings represented. What had been rebellion in her heart turned to appreciation. She was excited to go home to once again set her table using her napkin ring.

Since hearing this story, I want to implement this tradition in our family. It will cost money to invest in monogrammed napkin rings for all of my family members initially, but then each person will have

Educational Table Traditions Using Carry-In Meals

- Create a picnic in your family room by spreading a blanket on the floor. Serve Southern Fried Chicken and talk about southern culture in America.

- Serve Asian food and prepare a low table in the living room. Sit on cushions and eat with chopsticks. Read and discuss the Chinese proverb from the fortune cookie.

- Have a Mexican fiesta. Decorate your table with bright colorful objects, make paper mustaches for the guys' faces and paper flowers for the gals' hair. Speak Spanish if you can.

Learning the traditions of others and inventing your own create a lifetime of memories for your family.

his or her own special napkin ring to use and will remember the times we have enjoyed together at the table.

A Solitary Seat of Honor

I realize that some of you reading this book may not have a family around your dinner table. Your circumstances are such that in the evenings, you find yourself eating alone. If you live alone or are alone most of the evenings in your home, I urge you to set a solitary seat of honor at your table for yourself. Please don't eat your food while standing at the kitchen counter, and by all means, don't take it to the couch to eat while you watch TV. Instead, set a place at your table and experience the supernatural Bread of the Presence, who meets you there.

> Set a place at your table and experience the supernatural Bread of the Presence, who meets you there.

Mom Titus, my mother-in-love as I affectionately called her, was a very elegant lady—strong willed and determined, yet tender and kind. Her dry sense of humor kept us all laughing. Mom was very hospitable during her homemaking years, often inviting church families to their home for dinner. She loved to study the Word and taught Sunday school—usually a class of young married couples. These dynamic classes created a reputation in the community, and she began accepting invitations to speak at other church events in nearby towns.

Larry, my husband, is her youngest son. One memory of his mother is seeing her remain at the table after breakfast for most of the morning. This is where she did her Bible study.

When Larry went to college, Mom and Dad Titus traveled from church to church and state to state bringing life to dead religion and stuffy theology. A few years later, Dad passed away in his sleep. It was a sudden surprise to all of us—especially to Mom.

As traveling evangelists, hotels had been home to Mom and Dad Titus for several years. Her new life without Dad necessitated that she rent an apartment near us. This lady of strong faith and independent personality began struggling to adjust to living alone. Her lifestyle was dramatically interrupted, and she had a difficult time finding her way.

More than one year had passed, and Mom seemed to still be grieving. She shared with me that she simply could not make herself sit at the table to eat alone. The empty chair at the table was too stark a reminder to her of her beloved husband's absence. So she would make a sandwich and eat it in front of the television in the living room or in the recliner in her bedroom.

I encouraged Mom to buy fresh flowers, light a candle, and set a pretty place for herself at the table. "You deserve it," I said. Mom took my advice and began setting a solitary place at the table. Several weeks passed, and Mom said that she had begun to look forward to sitting at the table. She explained that she often received inspiration and insight for her Bible teaching there. Referring to the times when she experienced the

Terrific Table Talk

Honorable Conversation

- Compliment the person who sits in the seat of honor.

- Ask your honored guest to tell something special about him- or herself from a personal story in his or her past.

- Tell your honored guest why he or she is important to you.

- Share a story about you.

supernatural presence of Jesus at the table, she joked to others that she was dining regularly with "her wealthy Jewish husband." She became a new lady—a lady with a mission once again.

Prepare a Seat of Honor at Your Table

Who needs to be invited to a seat of honor in your sphere of influence? Is it a child or teenager who has no loving family to celebrate him? (Notice I did not say to celebrate *his special day*; I said to celebrate *him*.) Or is it a neighbor who has lost a job? It could be a friend going through a difficult and unwanted divorce or perhaps a colleague entering retirement. This list can go on and on. You may have a strained relationship with a son or daughter, a relative or friend. Regardless of the circumstances, giving people a seat of honor at the table can demonstrate your affection and respect for them more than a thousand words.

I encourage you to prepare a seat of honor at your table—first for each member of your family, and then for others whose personal dignity and sense of value will be enhanced because you invited them to your table. Doing this has been the joy of our lives, and it will be a delight to yours as well.

Table Reflections

1. Who in your life needs to be invited to a seat of honor in your home?

2. How do you think it made Mephibosheth feel when David declared, "You shall eat at my table regularly" (2 Sam. 9:7)?

3.   What can you add to your table setting to make your family feel valued?

4.   How will you honor each of your family members at your table? List the steps you will take.

5.   What statements of honor can you say to your family and guests while you are at the table?

Part 2

The Table Is a Place of Provision

Chapter 5
Our Daily Bread

Give us this day our daily bread.

—Matthew 6:11

THERE ARE NOT ENOUGH fingers on my hands to count the number of times I have determined to go on a diet after the beginning of a new year. It is so easy to put on pounds and so hard to take them off! With determination to break my eating-the-wrong-things-the-wrong-way habit, I always begin with a fast. I do not eat anything for twenty-four hours; I only drink water. Why do I do this? Because I want my mind to tell my body who is in control. I am saying to my physical body, in essence, "You are not going to dictate to me what I will do. I am in charge of you."

Yes, I get a headache when I fast because I love my morning coffee. And by the end of the day, my hunger cravings are screaming at me. My body is saying, "I know what I want, and I want it now!" We call these hunger pains. The longer we go without food, the more we are convinced that we were created to eat! Why do our bodies respond this way? Because God created our bodies to need food—and not just food; we also need other nourishing elements God designed to go with food, such as community and security and identity.

When Jesus' disciples observed how He prayed, they wanted to know how to follow His example. In the prayer Jesus taught His disciples, known today as the Lord's Prayer, He includes this phrase: "Give us this day our daily bread" (Matt. 6:11). This was a prayer for the provision of daily food. Why? Because daily food is essential to good health.

Have you ever thought about the fact that God designed our bodies in such a way that we need food every single day? He could have designed our bodies to eat once a month, or once a year. But because He knew that gathering at the table includes so much more than physical nourishment, He designed our bodies so that we have to eat every day of our lives. And not just once a day, but *three times a day*! Three times every day, God provides food to nourish our bodies. And three times every day, we have the opportunity to express our gratitude for His provision.

The Main Ingredient: Common Sense

As I approach this chapter, I do not pretend to be a nutritional expert. But I do want to talk to you in a practical "mom" way about using common sense when you prepare meals for your family. Just think about this for a minute. Whoever is responsible for preparing family meals contributes in a significant way to the overall physical health of the family. You can't consistently feed your family junk food, processed food, and sugary foods and expect them to be healthy!

Whoever is responsible for preparing family meals contributes in a significant way to the overall physical health of the family.

I know what some of you may be thinking as you read those words: *I don't have time to prepare healthy meals!* Preparing healthy meals does not have to be difficult, nor does it have to be expensive. In this chapter, I will present a simple approach to preparing healthy meals that I hope will make it easier for you. The table experience is not only about the food we eat, but it is also about our emotional, spiritual, and physical health.

Moms and dads, stop and think about this. When your babies were born, you instinctively knew that their growth and health depended on the nutrition that comes from milk. A mother either feeds her baby with breast milk or with manufactured milk designed to be very similar to the mother's milk. As parents, we understand that all our baby's vital organs depend on this nutrition. A few months later, we know to add grains, such as rice cereal and oatmeal, to our baby's diet. Then we gradually add fruits and vegetables. These foods are essential to the health of our mind and our body.

Why, then, when our children are older, do we stop frequently serving them whole grains, fruits, and yellow and green vegetables? It often seems that as soon as our children are able to feed themselves, we no longer serve them spinach and squash, oatmeal and milk, as if they have somehow outgrown these nutritious foods. Instead, we begin handing them pizza, hot dogs, and French fries. None of these items is bad for us by itself, of course, but if we want our bodies to stay healthy, we must eat these foods in moderation in addition to a diet rich in the fruits and vegetables, grains and protein that are necessary for the proper growth and health of growing vital organs.

With a little ingenuity and a lot of common sense, you can begin today to create meals that will enhance your family's growth and health.

With a little ingenuity and a lot of common sense, you can begin today to create meals that will enhance your family's growth and health.

Good Nutrition Starts at the Table

Before I share some specific ideas for preparing nutritious meals, let me emphasize again that healthy family meals begin at the table. You simply cannot monitor the portions or nutritional value of the foods your family eats when everyone grazes in the pantry at various times throughout the day and snacks on whatever they can find. The epidemic of expanding waistlines that we see today is partially a result of the constant availability of food! And you cannot supervise the healthy diet of teenagers who habitually buy something at the drive-through window on the way home from sports or band practice. The best way for you to encourage and supervise healthy eating patterns in your home is to gather your family to eat meals together at your table on a regular basis.

If you are like many people, your kitchen table is probably buried under all kinds of clutter—bills, homework, junk mail, laundry, and who knows what else! This is not to say that you cannot use your dining table for these kinds of purposes. After all, it's a great work space for scrapbooking and other projects. But when mealtime rolls around, don't use your cluttered table as an excuse to take your food into another room or to eat on the couch. Instead, take five minutes and clear the table! Find a place for those odds and ends, even if that means putting them in a box you store under the table. That way, even if your dining table serves as a science project lab or a home office during the days, you can set apart the table during evening mealtimes as a place for your family to eat and to converse.

Nutritionists tell us that we shouldn't eat all over the house. And especially we should not eat in front of the television! In 1988, researchers at the Children's Nutrition Research Center in Houston found that kids who were overweight ate 50 percent of their dinners in front of the television, while for normal-weight children, the number was 35 percent. Karen Cullen, behavioral nutritionist and assistant professor of pediatrics, says, "We know there's a link between the number of hours children watch television and weight problems. We also know that people who watch television while eating tend to tune out their natural hunger and satiety cues, which encourages overeating."[1] Plus, exposure to the messages on television contributes to poor nutrition. Cullen points out, "The foods most heavily advertised tend to be low in nutritional value."[2] Think about it: when was the last time you saw a commercial for broccoli or tossed salad? So when we eat in front of the television, our minds are being filled with appetizing visions of fatty, processed foods. And while our attention is focused on these messages, we keep reaching into that bag of chips, not realizing how much we are actually eating. This is very different than serving a proportioned amount of food on a plate at a table and then eating the meal with other people, all of whom are facing one another and interacting together.

> The best way for you to encourage and supervise healthy eating patterns in your home is to gather your family to eat meals together at your table on a regular basis.

Another reason we should have family meals at the table is because when eating is a social activity that happens at designated times in a specific setting, we are more likely to eat appropriate portions of food, thus reducing the risk of eating disorders and obesity. As Weinstein points out, "If we are served a reasonable portion, along with everyone else in the family, we learn what a moderate helping is. If we talk while we eat, we are less likely to eat as much as we can, as fast as we can."[3] When parents model eating nutritious foods in appropriate amounts as a normal part of everyday life, children are less likely to view food inappropriately or to eliminate entire food groups as a means of weight control, which can lead to eating disorders. Our kids learn from what we do, so if we skip meals, diet constantly, snack in front of the television, or starve all day and gorge ourselves at night, these are the kinds of eating habits our children will tend to adopt.

When we set aside time every day to eat a complete nutritious meal, we will have an overall healthier lifestyle. Marjorie Garber wrote, "Perhaps increasingly, for busy people, space has come to substitute for time, and the house becomes the unlived life. In an era when the 'welcome mat' and the 'answering machine' all-too-often stand in for personal greeting and the human voice, the house—with its 'living' room, 'dining' room, 'family' room and 'media' room, is the place where we stage the life we wish we had time to live."[4] We Americans have lots of space and no time—at least no time to do what is most important. We are starved, but not for food—we are starved for connection, meaning, conversation, and the Bread of the Presence. This is why coming together for the dinner experience at the family table is essential.

We are starved, but not for food—we are starved for connection, meaning, conversation, and the Bread of the Presence.

Making Good Food Fun

A return to the table can make good food fun. I encourage you to set the table with fun colors, dishes, and glasses. Colored straws and paper napkins are great for young families. Lovely linens and mats also make a table attractive. Most importantly, involve the children in the preparation for the meal. Hanging out in the kitchen creates unforgettable family memories. If you have toddlers, allow them to play with colorful and safe kitchen items, such as plastic spatulas or colorful plastic-ware while you prepare the meal. This will get them involved at a young age with the meal preparation process. When your children are school-age, you can assign simple jobs for them to help with, such as tearing lettuce for salad and counting out the forks from the drawer. Involve as many family members as you can in the process of making good food. Part of the fun of dinner is working together in the kitchen to get it prepared. Very young children love to help. There is always something to do. And older children should be included in the meal preparation as well.

Terrific Table Talk

Conversation—The Main Dinner Ingredient

- Create word games. Begin with a sentence and have each person create a story by adding another sentence. This will stimulate thinking skills while also cultivating laughter.

- Talk about a specific food item. How is it grown? Where it is grown? What are its nutrients?

- Talk about your day. You might ask two questions. What was the best thing that happened today? What was the most frustrating thing that happened today?

- Encourage children to express their viewpoint by asking, "What do you think about that?"

- Sing at the table. You can sing your prayer or finish the meal by singing something together.

Trina, our daughter, enjoyed helping me in the kitchen. Her usual assignment was to make the salad and to set the table. To this day, she sets a beautiful, fun, and creative table for her family of four children, their spouses, and her first grandchildren. The conversation at her family table is as lively as her table settings. After all, communication should be the main dinner ingredient!

Fresh Is Best

I was reared in California's Salinas Valley. Some called it the lettuce bowl of California. Rich, dark soil nourished most of our commonly known fresh vegetables: various kinds of lettuce, tomatoes, broccoli, cauliflower, strawberries, artichokes, asparagus, and many more. As children, we learned to recognize the crops as they were growing. Sometimes we played in the fields, getting wet and muddy in the irrigation ditches. We ate freshly picked iceberg lettuce straight from the field. There is no flavor like a fresh head of iceberg lettuce! We banged the core of the lettuce on our knee to loosen it. When we removed the core, into the hole our thumbs would go. With a snap of the wrist, we split open the crisp head of lettuce and crunched into it as if it were an apple. This is real food.

I understand that most of your children do not live in lettuce fields like I did. I'm only illustrating how good fresh food in its simplest form can taste. I'm convinced, if we start children out on real food—fresh food, fruit and veggies—they will learn to love their natural flavors.

I'm convinced, if we start children out on real food—fresh food, fruit and veggies—they will learn to love their natural flavors.

By the way, if you have children who have not yet developed a taste for fruit and vegetables, please do not use that as a reason to become a short-order cook and fix everyone in your family a separate meal according to his or her liking. Meals should be made according to nutritional value and parents' preference, and children will learn to enjoy the kinds of foods that are healthy for their growing bodies. If you have a picky eater at home, don't be discouraged! Research shows that it can take many exposures to a specific food before a person's taste buds adapt to the taste. And rest assured that taste is something that can be acquired. After all, who would drink coffee or eat jalapenos based on their taste buds' first reaction? Some studies suggest that it takes ten or more times of trying a new food before a person will learn to like it.[5] So if your children are reluctant to try new foods, don't let that deter you from serving them the nutritious foods their bodies need. Keep putting good food on their plates, and after a while, your children will eventually learn to like it.

My mom was a working mom, but she always had a home-cooked meal on the table. It was not necessarily gourmet; most of our meals were very simple and yet delicious. You could call it plain food or real food—steamed vegetables, sautéed or broiled meats, and rice or potatoes, both Idaho potatoes and yams. Sometimes beans would replace the meat. Our table was set with linens and dishes that weren't fancy, but they were colorful and coordinated. Mom usually prepared more than one vegetable, so we had a choice. Making us eat certain amounts was never an issue. Mom just did not want us to waste food by overserving our plates. She preferred that we finish eating what we took. But then, we were not allowed to snack shortly before coming to dinner.

In my own family's home, after we finished eating, Trina, Aaron, Larry, and I all helped with the dishes. While recently visiting our son's home, I noticed that Aaron naturally clears the table and helps clean the kitchen, very much like his dad did when he was growing up and continues even now. It is not uncommon after I prepare and serve a meal that Larry will say, "I'll do the dishes." We usually end up doing them together because I want to be in the kitchen with him. It's a time for us to talk and to enjoy being with each other.

When our children were growing up, being in the kitchen together often turned into a fun, playful time for us. Family memories of cleaning the kitchen include lightly popping each other with the damp dishtowels, chasing each other around the table, and other silly games as we enjoyed being together in the kitchen. When I was growing up, Mom was always making up games for my brother and me. For example, when we did the dishes, it was a race to see who could finish first. The person drying the dishes could stop if the dish drainer became empty. The person drying the dishes also had to clear the table. If the person washing ran out of dishes to wash, he could quit while the other had to finish cleaning the kitchen. This game kept Noel and me working rapidly.

Food Made Easy

We are so blessed to have so many products and services today that are available to help us prepare healthy meals quickly. For example, many of our local grocery stores include precut fruits and vegetables, along with a colorful tossed salad that is already prepared and bagged. The frozen food department often has real onions already diced and ready to pull out of the reclosable bag. No more dissolving into tears while slicing onions in your kitchen! These kinds of options make preparing healthy meals a lot easier for us.

Many working and otherwise busy moms enjoy the convenience of assembly kitchens, such as Super Suppers and Dream Dinners, along with similar businesses that specialize in making meal preparation easy. These businesses have recipes you can choose with fresh ingredients that are already chopped, grated, or shredded waiting for you to simply measure and assemble the meal. This meal can be frozen to be served at a later time. Within a couple of hours in one of these kitchens, you can make enough meals for your family for one week. That's one alternative.

Another alternative is to double or even triple the recipe each time you cook a meal. It might take you a few more minutes during your initial cooking session, but it will save a lot of time later. You can simply measure the extra servings into a separate container, such as a reclosable bag or disposable aluminum tray available in many grocery stores, label it with the recipe and date, and store it in your freezer to be reheated for dinner on a busy day. Soup, chili, and spaghetti and meatballs freeze great in a mason jar. Lasagna also does fine in a reclosable bag—just add fresh sauce when you reheat it.

> **Cook x 2=Another Meal**
>
> Cook two pounds of hamburger or two breasts of chicken instead of one.
>
> One for today. One for tomorrow.

One mother I know sets aside the first Saturday of each month to cook several meals at once and freeze them. For example, she'll cook five pounds of ground beef and then portion the cooked meat into various recipes—stuffed peppers, seasoned taco meat, and so on—and put those meals in the freezer. The next month, she'll bake or grill several pounds of chicken breasts at one time, and then she portions those into various casseroles and entrées. By setting aside one day a month to do several days' worth of cooking, she is able to serve her family home-cooked, nutritious meals, even on busy weeknights, by simply adding vegetables and bread.

Another meal preparation option is to simply cook fresh food like my mother did. I have followed in her tradition. Nothing wearies me more than trying to follow a recipe with twenty-five ingredients. Just give me real food and fresh herbs, cream, and butter, and I can give you a delicious meal.

I agree with Michael Pollen, author of *In Defense of Food*, as he distills what we should eat into seven simple words: "Eat food. Not too much. Mostly plants."[6] I love the premise of his book. Although his writing style is quite scientific, he intelligently defines a simple truth: "Most of what we are consuming today is not food, and how we are consuming it—in the car, in front of the TV, and increasingly alone—is not really eating. Instead of food, we're consuming 'edible food-like substances.'"[7]

Although we cringe at the words *edible food-like substances*, we often readily fill our pantries with boxed, processed foods whose ingredients we cannot even pronounce. You may ask, *How can I prepare meals without these quick aids?* I have good news for you— you do not have to. Just remember to use fresh ingredients as much as possible. For example, when buying ground beef for your quick "helper" dish, buy good-quality lean beef and serve a fresh vegetable on the side. Buy real butter, rather than imitation. When preparing boxed macaroni and cheese, add real cheese to the cheese-flavored powder to increase its nutritional value.

In our current world of nutritionists and the FDA regulations along with consumerism, real food has almost gone by the wayside. In our hurried lifestyles, we are eating fresh food less and less, especially if drive-through fast food has become your family's habit. Let me clarify here that I am not an organic extremist, digging my own potatoes in the backyard and raising my own chickens. However, I love real food, good food, simply prepared with herbs and spices. I think it's the easiest way to cook.

In my opinion, the best time-saving way to purchase food is to shop the peripheral aisles in your supermarket. You'll be in and out in half of the time. Along these outer aisles is where you'll find the good food: fruits, vegetables, cheeses, bakery breads, dairy, fresh pastas, and the like. You will also want to find the frozen food aisles because frozen foods are quick and easy to prepare, and many of them have preserved more vitamins than the canned foods, especially vegetables. Although you can freeze some of your own items, it is a time saver to have some already frozen foods on hand. Keep the less healthy snacks for a treat, not a regular meal replacement. When you buy breads, buy whole grain. I'm not sure my children ever knew that bread came in white!

Rate Your Plate

Even if you don't enjoy cooking or have little experience in putting together healthy meals, by following just a few simple tips, you can prepare a table and serve good food. For starters, rate your plate. See if you have provided something from each of the five food groups in your meal. Let's review the basic five food groups and how essential they are for good nutrition.

- Grain—provides energy
- Vegetable—improves vision
- Fruit—heals cuts
- Meat (protein)—builds strong muscles
- Dairy—builds strong bones/teeth

An easy way to plan your plate is to choose complementary colors of food on the plate. For example, your menu could look something like this:

Food Group	Food	Color
Meat	Sautéed Lemon-Peppered Chicken Breast	White
Vegetable	Baked Sweet Potato	Orange
Vegetable & Dairy	Steamed Broccoli with Melted Cheese	Green and yellow
Fruit	Waldorf Salad	White with red
Grain	Whole Grain Roll	Brown

A meal like this takes less than thirty minutes to prepare and provides a colorful and nutritious plate for your family. Whenever possible, avoid serving chicken breast with cauliflower, rice, apple salad, and roll with milk to drink. This menu has all five food groups, but it has no color. Everything is a shade of white. No one will find a meal like this exciting to eat.

Remember, cooking is an art, while baking is a science. Like art, when you cook, you have the freedom to create and make it your own. When you bake, you must follow the recipe. Maybe that is why I prefer cooking to baking—I love doing my own thing!

Quick tip: Avoid using recipes with lots of ingredients. Save these for the weekend when you want to try something new.

Start the Day Right

Our daily bread should begin with good thoughts. We know from science that a person's physical health is affected by his or her emotional health. Working in the kitchen together is a time to compliment and encourage, a time to celebrate accomplishments and to laugh at mistakes. Accidents will happen, so keep a package of Band-Aids handy!

Dr. Daniel G Amen, MD, explains that "every time you have a good thought, a happy thought, a hopeful thought, or a kind thought, your brain releases chemicals that make your body feel good." [8] Thoughts are powerful. They can make your mind and your body feel good, or they can make you feel bad. Every cell in your body is affected by every thought you have.

When you arise in the morning, think positive thoughts about the day. When you awaken your children, speak kind words to them.

Touch them gently and speak to them something positive about themselves. No one wants to wake up to a loud voice yelling, "Get up, now!" Speaking uplifting words in a gentle voice to each family member in the mornings will prepare them to eat a good breakfast before going to school for their day, ready to meet any challenge. This principle is the same for you and your spouse—a gentle answer, a positive voice, and a healthy breakfast can make a big difference in your day.

Breakfast is commonly known to be the most important meal of the day. It is called by some experts to be the brain food—that is, if it includes protein. A granola bar is not sufficient to begin a day with the best nutrition; it contains too much sugar and too many additives.

Researchers have also found that when we eat breakfast rich in natural carbohydrates such as whole grain cereals, along with a lean protein such as eggs, this can help maintain our mental performance over the morning, according to Dr. Phil McGraw in his book *Family First*. On a chart that he calls "Brain Foods for BrainPower," Dr. Phil outlines several foods and their benefit and function to the brain:

> Citrus: Foods such as oranges and grapefruits are high in vitamin C, which improves memory and performance.
>
> Eggs: Eggs are high in a memory-building vitamin called choline.
>
> Fish: Fish contains important brain-building fats.
>
> Green, orange, yellow, and purple fruits and vegetables: these foods are rich in antioxidants that can protect brain cells against damage, as well as potassium, which helps prevent mental fatigue.
>
> Lean meats (beef and poultry): These foods are high in iron; deficiencies in iron impair learning and memory.
>
> Whole-grain and iron-fortified cereals: These foods are excellent sources of carbohydrates, which are required for sharp mental performance.[9]

Add physical activity to all of this good food and positive thinking, and you will be well on your way to having a healthy family.

Working Moms Can Make Meals Too

Our son, Dr. Aaron Titus, is a physicist and an assistant professor at High Point University in North Carolina. So is his wife, Dr. Kimberly Titus. Although Kim chose to delay her full-time career while their two daughters were not yet in school, she tutored science and math students, programmed and tested textbook problems for online assessment, and taught math a few hours a day at her daughters' school. Now Kim is a full-time assistant professor in mathematics at the same university where Aaron is the department chairman of chemistry and physical science. They both have a lot of responsibility.

In addition to their career responsibilities, Aaron and Kim are volunteer leaders at their church. Together they teach Sunday school. Kim works in children's church and co-leads a mime troop. Aaron codeveloped and trains leaders for a small-groups system for their church, and Aaron and Kim host a small group in their home.

While they are very busy, you would not know it at mealtime. They have made eating dinner together a

Quick Tips for Working Moms

- *Pray* for your family while you prepare your meal.

- *Place* the Bread of the Presence on your table by asking Him to be among you.

- *Prioritize* your schedule so you set aside more than one day per week to have meals together at home at your table.

- *Plan* and make lists. List your menus and the ingredients you will need.

- *Prepare* your table by setting it in advance, preferably the day before. Prepare food in advance by using quick aids.

priority for their family. They balance their busy lives with peace because they come to the table together—where the presence of the Prince of peace is among them. For this reason, their relationships are strong, and their children are vibrantly healthy, both physically and emotionally, as their spiritual sensitivity continues to develop.

I have asked Kim, my awesome daughter-in-love, as I affectionately call her, to share a few of her tips and priorities for you.

Mealtime Tips from Dr. Kim Titus— A Professional Mom

Scheduling

The key to successful family mealtimes is to communicate with family members when planning a time for dinner. For all or most of you to be present at the same time, your mealtime may need to change from day to day. Who says dinner has to be at six o'clock sharp? If four thirty or seven thirty works for everyone, do it then. If your family dinner is scheduled for later than usual one evening, plan snacks for the kids as appropriate so they don't mind.

If your husband gets home after everyone has eaten, serve the rest of the family dessert when Dad eats so that you can be together at the table. Occasionally when Aaron has to work late, we've met him at a restaurant, even at an early time like four o'clock, just to see him and be together. At other times, we've packed a picnic or picked up a pizza or Chinese takeout and have taken dinner to his office!

In the last thirty to sixty minutes before dinnertime, call family members who are not yet home to check their EAT (estimate arrival time). If they are running late, don't start steaming the vegetables until they call you to say they are on their way home. Again, the important thing is not eating at a specific time, but eating together!

In our home, we always have an extra chair at the table. That way, instead of waiting for our children's friends to leave so that our family could eat together, we would invite their friends to join us at the table. We let them choose (or, when the children were younger, we would consult with their friends' parents) whether to eat a full meal or simply to sit with us while we ate dinner. Eating together doesn't have to be an exclusive event for only your family members. What a great experience for a child whose family doesn't share a meal together regularly!

Planning

Take a few minutes—not hours—to plan and shop each week. When you think through what is needed for a meal, you can stock up on essentials in a relatively short amount of time. What constitutes a meal? A serving of meat with a starch and raw or cooked vegetable is more than sufficient. Keep enough basic ingredients on hand for most of your favorite meals. Stock up on sides like rice, noodles, pasta salad mixes, macaroni and cheese, frozen vegetables, frozen garlic bread, and canned soup. I try not to let my stock get low, and I organize my pantry with new cans to the back so I use my oldest items first. Buying in bulk can save you money too. When your local supermarket has a buy-one-get-one-free special and it's double coupon week, it's time to stock up on that product! Chances are, your favorite product will be on sale once every four to eight weeks.

For easy meal preparation and cleanup, try a simple dish like stir-fry. Then steam rice, and you have a meal with only two pots to clean. Save new recipes for only those evenings when you have the time and energy. On those hectic and long days, stick to tried-and-trusted recipes that your family enjoys. And on days when you simply do not have time to prepare a meal at home, rotisserie chickens are great! Pick one up on your way home from church on

Sunday (half-price at my market), either to eat immediately or for a night when you'll get home late.

Take a look at your week and plan to have the easiest meal on your busiest afternoon or longest day. In our family, when I know I have a busy day coming up, I try to fix a large enough meal the night before so we can eat the leftovers the next day. But take my advice, from experience: if you decide to do this, be sure to communicate your plan to your family so that your precious leftovers don't disappear into lunchboxes or get eaten as a midnight snack!

Get your family excited about eating together by planning a night to pick up a pizza or their favorite carryout. Or treat yourself to a trip to Dream Dinners, Entré Vous, Super Suppers, Let's Dish, or other meal preparation service. Remember to take meat or frozen leftovers out of the freezer either the night before or the morning of to thaw. Thaw in the refrigerator to avoid food spoilage.

Preparation

Remember the CrockPot you received as a wedding gift but has been collecting dust in the back of your kitchen cabinet? Turns out, it's a wonderful invention after all! It takes only a few minutes in the morning to start a roast, soup, chili, or chicken pot pie in a slow cooker, let it simmer all day, and then dinner is done when you arrive home. Let a pork or beef roast (or two, if you need to have enough for leftovers) simmer all day in the CrockPot. They make delicious leftovers with a quick side of rice and veggies. Or shred the leftover roast for enchilada or burrito filling or add barbecue sauce for sandwiches.

When making tonight's salad, cut a few extra vegetables to make tomorrow's veggie tray. Store in a covered tray or shallow container to pull out as an appetizer as the family is arriving home and anxiously awaiting dinner. It's healthy and buys you a little time in which to prepare dinner.

Reborn meals—a fancy way to say reconstituted leftovers—are a great way to quickly put together a family meal. Last night's ground beef for tacos can be tonight's filling for enchiladas, burritos, or even lasagna. Enchiladas can be quick; you just warm a bag of corn tortillas, dip them in canned enchilada sauce, roll them up with meat inside, and place in a skillet with more sauce. Smother in cheese and cook until the cheese is melted. Be sure to double the recipe and prepare another pan to bake another night!

When we grill steak or chicken breasts for our family, we like to grill extra. In fact, we'll often grill a whole four-pound bag of chicken at one time! Some chicken breasts might be large enough to cut in half or even three pieces, which is a great way to monitor portion size, stretch your meal dollar, and facilitate meal planning. Reheat leftover chicken and steak and cut them in strips on top of a chef salad. Or cut the leftovers in strips and freeze them in a bag. On fajita night, dump the bag in a skillet with some sautéed fresh or frozen onion and pepper slices, and reheat for a few minutes. Or use the frozen strips of meat to make a Chinese stir-fry with a bag of frozen vegetables.

Let the kids help. They can set the table, fetch the salad dressing, stir the rice, make the brownies you'll bake during dinner, and help serve. It will get dinner on the table faster, and it just might distract them so they may momentarily forget how hungry they are!

Thank you, Kim, for your very practical guidelines. The healthy living values your family experiences at home will influence their choices for a lifetime. Proverbs 24:3–4 tells us, "By wisdom a house is built, and by understanding it is established; and by knowledge the rooms are filled with rare and beautiful treasures." Each family member is your rare and beautiful treasure, so use wisdom as you understand these principles and make the adjustments needed so that your daily bread brings life to all who partake.

Table Reflections

1. List the four thoughts that Dr. Amen identifies that releases brain chemicals that make you feel good.

2. Fill in the blank the remaining words that complete the seven simple words Michael Pollen uses to guide us in what we should eat: Eat_____; not too_____; mostly_____.

3. List three inspirations from the guidelines of Dr. Kim Titus, a professional mom, that will make meal preparation easier for you.

4. Rate your plate. What colors do you need to add to your usual menus to improve the nutritional value of the dinners that you do prepare? Which food group is missing?

5. List healthy thoughts that you can add to your healthy meals to enhance healthy living.

Chapter 6
A Table Prepared for Us

God is gently calling you from the jaws of trouble. He is calling you to an open place of freedom. There he has set your table full of the best food.

—Job 36:16 ICB

THE CONFERENCE ROOM WAS filled with approximately two hundred women. With passion and conviction, I spoke on the table principle.

Immediately following the message, a lady pressed her way through the crowd to talk to me. She explained that she was a pastor's wife who had known of my ministry for twenty-five years. With admiration, she affirmed me and then told me her sad story. She was divorced from her pastor husband, and her sons were struggling with addictions and the difficulties that go with that lifestyle.

After hearing the convincing message on the significance of the table and the supernatural presence that rests among family members as they join there, the woman reflected to ten years earlier when their busy lifestyles full of church programs began squeezing out their family meals together. She realized that this was also the time that her family relationships began disintegrating. The day she heard me teach about the table principle in Scripture, she recognized what had gone wrong in what she and her husband thought was a good life.

With tears rolling down her face, she recalled that when her family stopped eating together, they stopped talking to one another. They stopped knowing what the next day's schedule for each of them would be, and they disconnected. At first, the family disconnected from her husband, the children's dad. He was very busy with church meetings and ministry responsibilities during the evenings, so he seldom came home for dinner. Because he was not there, she and the boys would help themselves to whatever they wanted. Before long, they no longer ate at the same time. Slowly, she witnessed her boys becoming relationally distant. Their bonding with their parents was interrupted, and emotionally they shut down. She tried to reach into their hearts but had no success. They simply stopped talking to one another. The family eventually fell apart. Until hearing me speak on the table principle, she had not been able to pinpoint when or why things began deteriorating. Now she knew.

The woman went on to say that she was in a new marriage, and her second husband was also a pastor. They had begun their relationship without eating meals together and so far had not seemed to connect with the intimacy that both of them desired. After hearing the message of God's design for the table, however, her new goal was to set her table and allow the supernatural presence of God to do His work in their relationship. I have heard from her since, and she is one happy lady and so is her husband. They have connected in intimacy of conversation and love for each other. They did not know what was missing in their relationship until they realized that the table was missing. Now she delights in setting her table, and they both delight in sitting at the table!

Emotional Stability Is Established at the Table

The common saying "It's the little foxes that spoil the vine" is actually a paraphrase of the wise instruction of King Solomon, who said, "Catch the foxes for us, the little foxes that are ruining the vineyards, while our vineyards are in blossom" (Song 2:15). While our vineyards are in bloom, our lives seems to be flowing smoothly—the marriage and the money have no tension, the children are doing good in school, we have no traumatic trials in our lives, and we enjoy what we are doing at our church. This was the case of the family described above. Yet the little foxes of business and complacency ruined the vineyard of their family and spoiled the blooms in their lives. If we do not trap these little foxes as they enter, they can eventually spoil our vineyards—our homes. I have identified two "little foxes" for you to be aware of as you prayerfully examine your life and your family.

Little Fox #1: Too Busy Doing Good Things

It is not the wrong things we are doing that are spoiling our quality time together. Often our days become stressful and frustrating because we are doing too many good things.

> Often our days become stressful and frustrating because we are doing too many good things.

A decade of research points to a positive family meal experience as the most significant event in the family for the emotional development of the children. In 1997, the American Psychological Association published a study that illustrated the crucial role of the family meal in lives of teenagers. The study found that adjusted teens—those with better relationships with their peers, more academic motivation, and few, if any, problems with drugs and depression—ate dinner with their families an average of five days a week.[1]

Dr. Chris Stout, former president of the Illinois Psychological Association and chief of psychology at Forest Hospital in Des Plaines, IL, points to the family meal's main ingredient—communication—as one key to raising emotionally healthy children. He says, "Tricky subjects, such as problems with peers or schoolwork, are more easily approached across the dinner table."[2] Other research by the University of Minnesota and the University of North Carolina showed similar findings: drug use, sex, violence, and emotional stress were less likely in households where the parents were present at crucial times, particularly during meals.[3]

Excessive activity is a "little fox" that will slowly spoil the "vineyard" of the emotional connection of the family. The essential aspects in the human heart—learning, connecting, and relating, which bring security and significance—seem to be directly related to the family meal. When we are running to and from activities, we have very little meaningful conversation and spend time disconnected from one another, isolated in our own interests. This can become unhealthy for two reasons. First, we tend to disconnect emotionally because we are together less. Second, isolation leads to less positive talking and less touching with affirmation, two main positive human emotional connectors.

If your family is not gathering regularly for family meals, ask yourself, *what am I doing that is more important than having a meal with my family? What am I sacrificing in order to do what I want to do?* You must prioritize your time. We all have the same amount of time to get the best outcome in the relationships we have with our family and friends.

Little Fox #2: Negativity

There is a direct correlation between our emotional health and our biological brain. I'm amazed to discover that at the table during family meals we can actually either tear down and weaken the biological health of the brain, negatively affecting its ability to process and assess information or we can strengthen its capacity to learn and assimilate information that will heal the mind from other forms of attack.

Dr. Daniel G. Amen, MD, a clinical neuroscientist, child and adolescent psychiatrist, and medical director of the Amen Clinic for Behavioral Medicine, clearly defines with the use of the SPECT brain scan that consistent negativity can break down cells in the human brain. In his book *Change Your Brain, Change Your Life*, Dr. Amen says, "Your brain is the hardware of your soul."[4] Your soul is the essence of who you are. What the human soul becomes is largely influenced by what the mind intakes from the interaction of the family. As we begin to understand this, we can begin to measure and evaluate what we say to one another in our homes. Ask yourself, "Do I speak to my spouse and children from a negative perspective or a positive one?"

> What the human soul becomes is largely influenced by what the mind intakes from the interaction of the family.

My mother, now eighty-five years old and still bright and active, has always been very emphatic about being positive. When I was young, she did not allow me to say, "I can't." If I really was incapable of doing something, she would make me rephrase my "I can't" to, "Perhaps someday I will be able to." Do you notice that slight difference? Both statements mean the same thing, but one is negative and one is positive.

Chapter 3 in Dr. Amen's book clearly defines the "deep limbic system of the brain," as he has called it. This term is his term, simplifying the complexities of the limbic system in laymen's terms which have become helpful for explanation. This is the system in the brain that is the approximate size of a walnut, positioned near the center of the brain. He identifies that this system is where love and depression function. It sets the emotional tone of the mind. This is where highly charged emotional memories are stored; it also controls appetites and sleep cycles. Although there are other listed functions of this power-packed walnut-sized piece of our mind, I will not list them for the sake of emphasis. The negative symptoms of the deep limbic system are: moodiness, irritability, social isolation, clinical depression (being the most extreme), negativity in general, negative perception of events, increased negative thinking, and decreased motivation. Most of these weaknesses are caused by the interruption of bonding. "Bonding and limbic problems often go hand in hand," says Dr. Amen.[5]

When the table becomes a high priority for us—whether we are married or single, with children or without children—something powerful happens within our minds. Keeping conversation positive, uplifting, and edifying is healthy for you and others who are sharing your meal. Your conversation will have the power to rebuild brain cells and perhaps even help a clinically depressed person along their road to recovery.

Keeping conversation positive, uplifting, and edifying is healthy for you and others who are sharing your meal.

Paul writes in his letter to his friends in Philippi, "Whatever is true, whatever is honorable, whatever is right, whatever is pure, whatever is lovely, whatever is of good repute, if there is any excellence and if there is anything worthy of praise, let your mind dwell on these things" (Phil. 4:8). My paraphrase of this verse is simple: find something positive in every person and everything, and make your thoughts dwell there.

You may have heard it said that our thoughts become our words, our words become our actions, our actions become our habits, and our habits become our character. I would finish this thought by declaring that our character becomes our destiny. If we want our families to experience emotional healing and strength, it is very important to create a table atmosphere of positive, uplifting conversation. This type of conversation will improve our habits, our character, and our destiny—who we become.

Terrific Table Talk

Create a Compliment

- Define the word *compliment*.

- Give an example of a compliment.

- Speak a compliment about each member of the family.

- Take turns going around the table and complimenting each family member.

Eleanor Roosevelt said, "Great minds discuss ideas; average minds discuss events; small minds discuss people."[6] This saying assumes that the talk about others is not edifying. Let this be a general rule around your table. Prepare a positive atmosphere for your dinner experience. If you speak about another person, be sure that your words are always complimentary and uplifting. This type of conversation begins with positive thoughts, which builds every cell in the body.[7]

Emotional Healing During Difficult Times

The first church Larry served as pastor grew large very quickly. Although we were young and inexperienced, Larry and I were passionate and enthusiastic and had lots of energy to see young people who were disillusioned with institutionalism, especially in the church, come to know a personal Jesus. Thousands worshiped together in our small central Washington town, and the creativity of ministry from this place influenced the nation. We developed elementary and high schools and a college of Christian arts, in addition to a radio station, bookstore, and *Virtue* magazine.

It all came to a screeching halt one day when we discovered misappropriation of funds and other improprieties. In a matter of days, our seemingly perfect world crashed. My husband went into a deep depression that led us to soon resign and relocate.

Our daughter, Trina, was in the ninth grade and our son, Aaron, was in the fourth grade when we moved to another state. Understanding the high visibility of our ministry and the dark pain that our family was in, a loving pastor asked us to come be part of his church and heal. Our story was different than the typical. We had done nothing wrong, but we had to assume the responsibility of what went wrong.

Larry's deep state of depression released in him fear, negativity, and a loss of hope. It was as if I lost my visionary husband of strong faith and now lived with someone I did not know. He was emotionally shut down and relationally distant. I had an overwhelming sense of responsibility to ensure that our children would not be daunted in their faith or in their confidence in the church. Neither did I want them to feel the pain of their father's distress. We moved out of state into a temporary apartment and then to a rental home. We had left everything we owned behind, except some of our essential pieces of furniture. There was just enough room for our small, round table in the kitchen of the rental house we called home.

I will never forget huddling around our table, night after night, talking to Trina and Aaron about the adjustments of the new school, a new neighborhood, and going to a new church where Dad was not the pastor. None of this was familiar. We felt the presence of our enemy on every side. We were blamed, misunderstood, and shamed.

Even during this difficult transition in our lives, we continued our family tradition of eating meals at the table. Early in the morning we ate breakfast before school; after school, we had cookies and milk at the table. Then we set the table for supper. It was as if we didn't want to leave the table. Although Larry didn't talk much during these meals, we were still together. I tried to keep the conversation light and positive despite our difficult and frustrating circumstances. Leaving the very busy lifestyle of the pastorate to face quiet days of loneliness and despair with an unknown future was very daunting. I am convinced that the thing that held us together as a family during that difficult transition was our time together at the table.

In the Presence of My Enemies

In Psalm 23, David reflects on God's loving, tender care for him— as a shepherd tends to his sheep. After he describes how God leads him, restores him, and guides him daily, David makes this interesting observation: "He *prepares a table for me* in the presence of my enemies" (v. 5; emphasis added).

Who are your enemies in your everyday life? Are they people you work with who want your position? Could your enemy be a relative, neighbor, or teacher? You might even feel that you live with your enemy. No matter who you are or what position you hold in life, I can almost guarantee that there is someone in your life who feels to you like your enemy.

What does an enemy want to happen to us? An enemy's objective is to press on us and cause us to retreat. I think we will all agree that no matter how many other wonderful, caring people are surrounding us, we can *feel* the presence of our enemies.

When I was seventeen, I married a pastor and was immediately immersed in the culture of the church. I didn't grow up in pastoral ministry, so I didn't know what to expect. Now, after more than forty years in ministry, when I think of my enemies, unfortunately, I think of the church. In our early days of ministry, there was a person in our church who, for whatever reason, did not like me. I mean, he *really* did not like me. The church we were pastoring had more than two thousand people, and I never knew which service he was coming to. But whenever he showed up, despite the 1,999 other people in the congregation, I could feel the presence of my enemy.

What did that feeling make me want to do? Remember, our enemy's objective is to be so aggressive that we come to a place where we want to retreat, pull back, and then eventually quit. During that time when I could feel the presence of my enemy in church, I really wanted to quit. And there have been other times when Larry and I could have easily quit and never returned to vocational ministry. The enemy of our souls wants us to draw back a little—in faithfulness, in ministry, in serving our husbands and families. Just step back a little, and then a little more, until we get to a place where we want to quit!

And it's during those times—the times when you, like David in the Psalms, feel that the presence of your enemy is absolutely intolerable—that Jesus says to you, in essence, "Come here, my dear child. I know things are hard for you. I see what's happening to you and how your enemy is conspiring against you, pressing you down and trying to get you to draw back. But don't quit! I've prepared a place for you at the table. Come over here and eat with me, and we'll go through this together." Even when your circumstances have not changed—the circumstances that are so distressing that you want to quit—Jesus wants you to know that you are His. When your enemies are pressing you down and causing you to draw back, Jesus brings you to the table. And at the table He says to you, "No matter what they're saying and no matter what you're feeling, you matter to Me. You are important to Me."

> When your enemies are pressing you down and causing you to draw back, Jesus brings you to the table.

We are not the only ones in the presence of our enemies every day. Our children are in the presence of their enemies every single day. There is always someone who is smarter, faster, and more talented. Whether in the classroom, on the playground, or sadly, even in the church, they are called degrading names by others, made fun of, and humiliated. But when your children come home from school or their activities, often there is no one home to greet them. The kitchen is dark and the oven is cold. There is no "prepared table" for them. Already feeling like a failure, our children come home to an empty house, get themselves something to eat alone, with no conversation, and escape at the computer or television with no opportunity to be encouraged and to process what they are feeling.

Maybe Mom is out doing good things. Maybe she's working at a significant job, volunteering at church, or leading a Bible study. But when her children come home, still reeling from the presence of their enemies, there's no one home to say, "What happened to you today, honey? Oh, I'm so sorry to hear that. Well, that teacher just doesn't realize how smart you really are! You are not alone, sweetie. We will be here for you, and we'll help you go through this." Your children desperately need to hear that, to have that built into their lives. And where do you have that conversation? Not at the drive through! No, you talk to your kids like this *at your table*. These kinds of conversations take place at home, face-to-face, at a place for them set at your table.

Perhaps it is you or your husband who comes home pressed beyond measure, discouraged and defeated, exhausted and ready to give up. Husbands, no matter what kind of job they have, are in the presence of their enemies at work. And they come home with worries and questions, such as, "Am I going to be able to provide for my family? Will I get that promotion the other guy is vying for? The company is downsizing...am I going to be next?" He comes home tired and discouraged and beaten down by his enemies, and what does he come home to? An empty kitchen. If he's lucky, there are some cold leftovers in the fridge for him to heat up for himself.

If the Good Shepherd prepares a table for us when we need courage to face another day and not to quit, the least we can do for our family members is to prepare a table for them in the presence of their enemies. We never know when we begin a day, what that day may bring to us. If it is discouragement, coming to the table with the Bread of the Presence can give new perspective and fresh energy to face our disappointments and to try again, love again, live again. Somehow, just sitting and relaxing at a prepared table can calm your spirit and make the next day worth facing.

Larry and I did not quit. We drew strength from one another at the table and didn't realize what was keeping us together. It was the supernatural presence that saw our potential and would not let us give up. A few months later, we accepted the invitation to pastor another congregation. We moved again and started all over. We are better for this trial in our lives, because Larry and I chose to be positive and stick together. I continued to set the table and kept a routine in our daily lives. Our kids did not grow bitter or rebellious, withdrawn or secluded, and neither did we. My husband rose to a new place of faith and leadership and together we continue in passionate, innovative ministry, bringing a personal message of love and peace to others.

> If the Good Shepherd prepares a table for us when we need courage to face another day and not to quit, the least we can do for our family members is to prepare a table for them in the presence of their enemies.

If I Can Do It, You Can Do It Too

Your story is very different than mine. But nonetheless, all of us encounter huge pressures and changes that we did not plan. A friend of mine titled her book *The Unintended Journey*. Her unintended journey was discovering her Christian husband's addiction to pornography.[8] Another friend's unintended journey was facing bankruptcy from their affluent lifestyle. My daughter's unintended journey, discussed more fully in chapter 9, was to discover her husband's extramarital affair. We all have unintended journeys in our lives—yours may have been an unwanted divorce, a death of a loved one, or a fearsome diagnosis.

These are the times in our lives when the last thing we want to do is to go to the store and buy new placemats and napkins, staple new fabric on our worn kitchen chairs, and plan to make meals at home. This certainly is not when you feel like browsing through cookbooks for ideas to make menus for the month. However, you can strengthen your family members and yourself by sharpening your focus on what happens at your table during this difficult time. In the face of hopelessness, in the presence of your enemies, the Bread of the Presence can turn your mourning into dancing and your sorrows into joy during your dinner experience (Ps. 30:11).

> Making meals for your family in the face of adversity creates stability for everyone.

Making meals for your family in the face of adversity creates stability for everyone. It creates an environment for the family to talk. What you eat is not the most important factor. When you are discouraged, you generally lose your creativity. Depression causes your energy and ambition to wane. When you feel this way, follow these few suggestions to keep mealtime a priority. This is when the food should be simple and the environment colorful! Here are a few simple ideas to get you started:

1. Set your table with bright colors, even if it is paper products, and play lively music during the meal as a background.

2. Plan to make someone laugh. "A joyful heart is good medicine, but a broken spirit dries up the bones" (Prov. 17:22). If you don't particularly feel funny, read a joke.

3. Ask questions that encourage conversation.

4. Bring family members their favorite food from a takeout restaurant.

5. Begin each meal with a prayer from your heart.

6. Prioritize your daily activities to eat meals together.

7. Use your best dishes and glasses one night. (Even dollar store stemware dresses up a table.) The family will feel special, especially when times are tough.

These simple steps will strengthen the emotions of the each family member as you walk through difficult times together. Remember, every problem in this life is temporary. It will not last forever.

Personal Identity

The dinner experience creates a sense of personal identity. This identity can stay with us for the rest of our lives. We can feel secure about ourselves or we can believe that we have no value, based on what happens or does not happen at the table.

I remember one evening, years ago, when a weathered-looking woman, slight in frame, with shoulder-length dark, curly hair came up to me after I spoke at a conference to tell me her story. She was creatively dressed with several unmatched layers, and her expressions were both dramatic and withheld. I could tell that her natural outgoing personality was held back by her personal uncertainty. Through tears and great distress, she described the horror of her childhood table experience. She twisted her tattooed hands as she talked, occasionally batting at the dripping tears on her face.

One year before her thirteenth birthday, her mother had remarried. She was so excited to have a daddy again. Most of her life had been without one, and she thought she would be like her friends who had what she thought was a normal family. A few weeks after she came to live with him, something happened she will never forget. It was at the table. Just the three of them were there: her mother, stepfather, and her. With glaring eyes and pursed lips, he looked at her and told her how ugly she was. He emphatically said that he could not eat with her presence at the table, declaring that her ugliness ruined his appetite. This precious young girl was sent from the table and was never allowed to eat at the table when he was present again. Her mother sat her place somewhere else in the house or at the table after he was finished eating.

Not long after that disgraceful exchange, she ran away from home. Dumpsters provided her winter warmth, and occasional stints of living in the house of a man who had rescued her gave her temporary significance. She had bounced from pillar to post for years.

This petite lady with delicate fine features and curly hair was emotionally damaged at the table by a cruel stepfather. She never felt significant again. That is, until she came to the table of the Lord. At forty-five years old, after a destructive lifestyle, her life was being renewed. A friend invited her to church and then to her home for dinner. She began learning how much she was loved by God and how lovely she really is. She had been emotionally destroyed at the table by the spirit of hate, but she was emotionally healed at the table by the spirit of love. This beautiful lady found her true identity in Christ at the table.

Jesus Himself was criticized for eating with sinners. The Pharisees, the religious elite of the day, slighted Jesus by calling him a "friend of tax collectors and sinners" (Matt. 11:19). When Jesus ate with tax collectors and prostitutes, He became one of them, so the Pharisees said. Of course, Jesus was not a sinner but truly a friend eating with friends, whether they were believers or not. He knew His presence of love and acceptance at the table would eventually transform their lives.

The redemptive presence of Christ at the table not only can heal those who are emotionally wounded, but it can also confirm and stabilize personal identity during difficult or confusing family circumstances. For example, your family may be a nontraditional family: a blended family, a single-parent family, a kids-only-on-the-weekends family. Your family may bring traditions and identities from generational backgrounds and sometimes very different racial or ethnic or religious backgrounds. Regardless of your specific circumstances, it is at your table that your new family will gain a sense of identity. New traditions and values can be implemented at the table. Affirmation and compliments will give others the courage to be vulnerable and to connect with their new family. Positive, uplifting conversation will encourage the blending of values and priorities.

> The redemptive presence of Christ at the table not only can heal those who are emotionally wounded, but it can also confirm and stabilize personal identity during difficult or confusing family circumstances.

One blended family shared with me that it was the husband's tradition to pray at the table, but her teenagers were not accustomed to praying before they ate. When the newly blended family sat down to their meal, picked up their forks and started to eat, their new stepfather at the head of the table sensitively let them continue. He did not want to embarrass them, but during dinner, he explained that in their new family, he wanted to pray before they eat. He allowed everyone to ask questions and to discuss the reasons for this change in their lifestyle. This man wisely began reshaping values and traditions at their table, and the family began to embrace their new identity.

My Father's Family Table

Dad was reared in a large family of ten children on a small farm in southeastern Oklahoma. It was the early part of the twentieth century. The family was very poor. I once asked Dad how he had such good character despite such a difficult childhood. He answered, "We didn't have things or education, but we had a lot of love. And Mama always had a meal on the table." In a house that was small for this family of twelve, my daddy's family always ate at the table. In spite of crowded space and shared beds, there was room in his house for the all-important table.

Something supernatural transpired in Dad's family while eating together every day—and often more than once a day. It was at the prepared table that their characters were being shaped. The security of their parents' love was being deeply embedded in these children's emotions. When the children were arguing over who would get the final serving of corn, their parents taught them to share. Everyone had a portion. The older children helped the younger ones as they washed dishes together. My daddy and his brothers and sisters learned responsibility at the table. And all of them, including my grandparents, eventually committed their lives to Jesus Christ.

My Mother's Family Table

In my mother's family, Grandpa was clearly the head of the household. After the death of his father, he assumed the responsibility of providing for his mother and younger siblings as well as for his own wife and five children. They all lived together. Grandpa farmed and worked on state road construction, and he was almost always home for dinner at night.

Their dining table was large and fed many people. They also regularly provided lodging for visiting preachers and travelers. They were hospitable to their neighbors on nearby farms. My mother's dinner experiences included prayer, meals, laughter, instruction, Bible studies, and family games. The table was the center of their home activity. Character, courage, and discipline were demonstrated around their table. Faith, hope, and love were given to everyone who shared meals with them.

As you can see, Mom's family table was very different from Dad's family table. However, the results of regularly eating together at their tables led to emotionally healthy children.

Our Family Table

Seldom do Larry and I visit our adult children's homes that they do not have guests there for dinner. Sometimes I think, *I wish we could just visit them without others here!* But then I remember this is the way our family table was when they were growing up. Why should I expect anything different in their families and homes? Their family tables are places of joy and refuge for others in the same way ours was.

When Trina and Aaron were young, we usually brought a family home for dinner after church on Sunday. Because we lived far away from our extended families, we always invited to our holiday tables others who had no special place to go. Men from prison, teens from the streets, celebrities, preachers, missionaries, relatives, parishioners—people from all walks of life have eaten at our table. Larry often brought folks home with him for dinner with or without advance notice. This was our way of life. In our more than forty years of marriage, Larry and I have had literally hundreds of people join us at our table.

At our family table, our children learned to serve others, to be courteous, and to converse with adults. Now that they are both grown and have families of their own, Trina and Aaron are hospitable and use their homes to love people and allow God to work in their lives while serving them a meal, a bowl of popcorn, or a simple glass of tea. Presently, we see these same hospitable values repeated in the home of our adult grandchildren. Our way of life has become their way of life—giving life to others from our families' tables.

There is always a place for you at the table.

Friends come and go, different phases of life come and go, but the tradition of the family table, where the Bread of the Presence meets us, doesn't change. There is always a place for you at the table. His presence is waiting for you there. Why don't you join Him?

Table Reflections

1.   Name the two foxes that can spoil your dinner experience.

2.   Paul said, "Let your mind dwell on these things" (Phil. 4:8). Read this verse and list the things that Paul said we are to allow our minds to dwell on.

3.   What does Jesus do on the days that you feel like quitting? What should you do for your family on their most troubling days?

4.   List three of the seven recommended colorful things that you can do at the table when the day may have been dreary for someone.

5.   List three special things you can do during difficult days to make your family feel loved, safe, and secure.

Chapter 7

"Remember Me"

The Lord Jesus in the night in which He was betrayed took bread; and when He had given thanks, He broke it and said, "This is My body, which is broken for you; do this in remembrance of Me." In the same way He took the cup also after supper, saying, "This cup is the new covenant in My blood; do this, as often as you drink it, in remembrance of Me." For as often as you eat this bread and drink the cup, you proclaim the Lord's death until He comes.

—1 Corinthians 11:23–26

WHEN JESUS KNEW THE days of His ministry on earth were drawing to a close, He gathered with His closest friends around a table to share a meal—a meal often called the Last Supper.

This was the Passover dinner, which, as we saw in chapter 2, was the most celebrated meal of the Jewish year. The people of Israel prepared this special meal every year as a way to remember God's miraculous intervention to save the Israelites from slavery in Egypt. But this meal was also central to Jesus' purpose. He had something important to tell His disciples, and He wanted them to experience His presence in a tangible way that night—at the table.

Like any dinner table, the table for the Last Supper was set with plates and cups and bowls. And on those dishes were the natural elements—bread and wine—that had been part of the Passover meal for centuries. Bread and wine were a regular part of daily meals during Jesus' time, and during this meal, He took those natural elements and used them for a very important purpose.

After interactive conversation during the meal, Jesus took the bread and broke it. The bread used in the Passover meal was unleavened, meaning that it was flat, like a cracker. So when Jesus broke the bread, it probably snapped apart in two jagged pieces. He held up that broken piece of *matzo*, the Hebrew name for their bread, in front of His disciples and said what I imagine meant something like this: "See these jagged edges? This is what My body is going to look like tomorrow. You're not going to want to look at it; you're not going to want to go to the cross and witness what will be done to Me. It's going to be brutal. Most of you will want to run. You'll want to hide. But I want you to know as you watch this happen to Me, don't be angry at the soldiers or hate Pilate for the brutality you will see. Don't blame the rabbis; it's not because of them that this is happening. What you are seeing is My body being broken for *you*. I'm doing this for you. Trust Me now; you will understand later."

Then Jesus picked up the cup, and He said something like this: "See this wine? This deep red wine; it's kind of the color of blood, isn't it? I want you to know that tomorrow, you are going to see more blood than you thought could flow out of a human body. But when you see My blood poured out for you on that cross, when my side will be pierced with a spear, I want you to know it's the sign of the new covenant I am making with you. I will die, but I will never leave you. I know this is hard to understand now; it seems impossible. But you will see and one day you will remember what I am saying to you. In fact, I want you to remember Me, to remember what I am going to do for you. I want you to know that you can always come to Me; even after I go away."

Then He told His disciples something really interesting: "Do this in remembrance of Me." I ask you, what did Jesus mean when he said, "Do this . . ." Do what? What were they doing while he was talking to them and giving them an illustrated life lesson? They were eating a meal together. What did He want us to remember? Hope! Redemption! That no matter what happens, He can fix it; He can heal us. He wants us to remember that He has provided for us.

And how often did Jesus want us to "do this," to remember His redemption? As often as we take communion, once a month in church? I don't think so. As I've been studying this passage in context of the table principle woven throughout the pages of Scripture, I think when Jesus held up that bread and that cup and said, "Do this in remembrance of Me," He was referring to eating dinner. In other words, He was saying, "As often as you eat bread and wine, remember that these elements represent My body and My blood, which I have given to redeem you." How often did Jesus' disciples eat bread and wine? Every single day, because those were the foods that were essential in life and served at every meal. Every time we come to the table, no matter what the circumstances, we are to remember that old things can change to new things. We are to remember that there is redemption for everything negative that we experience. He can make all things new.

Can you imagine what would happen in our homes if every time we ate a meal, it was at the table and our prayer was redemptive?

Can you imagine what would happen in our homes if every time we ate a meal, it was at the table and our prayer was redemptive? If every time we shared a meal together, we remembered Jesus' sacrifice and acknowledged His continual, supernatural presence at our table? Just think of how our families and our own lives would be transformed if every time we ate bread and wine—or any of the other natural elements of our meals today—we remembered the redemptive presence of Christ.

Table Prayers

"Thank You, Jesus, for this food. Bless it to our bodies. In the name of Jesus, Amen." Let's eat!

That's the type of prayer many Christians say at the table. Others have shortened their table prayers to something like this: "God is great; God is good. Let us thank Him for this food." I even know one pastor who, when Larry and I were guests for dinner at his home, tried to be funny and announced at the table, "Let's just eat. The food is already blessed. We just bless all the bags of groceries when we bring them home from the store!"

This is not what Jesus told us to do. Jesus said as often as we gather together at the table, He wants us to remember His plan for redemption, every day of our lives. Every time we eat a meal, we are to acknowledge His redemption of us. So our table prayers should not only express gratitude for God's provision, but they should also contain a message of redemption. No blanket blessings over the food in grocery store bags, and no halfhearted "Rub-a-dub-dub, thanks for the grub"!

Jesus said as often as we gather together at
the table, He wants us to remember His plan
for redemption, every day of our lives.

I'm not saying that our table prayers have to be complicated or dripping with theology. If your kids are very young, you could say a simple prayer that contains a redemptive message, something like, "Thank You, Jesus, that we can come around the table and know that when we make a mistake, we can tell each other about it and You can help us to know how to do it better next time." Can you see the message of redemption in that simple prayer? Just imagine: if children experience this type of content in table prayers from the time they are in the high chair, they will learn in a very natural way the power of God's redeeming love in their lives. This will build incredible self-esteem and confidence with humility. Our children will learn of God's love from the family table before they even go to Sunday school!

Your table prayer should always include expressing gratitude for what Jesus has done for you on the cross, rather than merely thanking Him for the food you eat. Remember, mealtime is not just about food, because "Man does not live on bread alone, but on every word that proceeds from the mouth of God" (Matt. 4:4). Let your prayer words be worthy of God. While the daily food He provides us is important, and we do need to express gratitude for God's abundant provision for us, it is far more important for our table prayers to acknowledge the purpose of the cross, God's love, and His redemptive presence with us at the table.

Learning to Pray at the Table

When I was growing up, our family table was normally set for four, and usually more. Dad sat at the head of the table, and Mom sat on his right. My older brother and I usually sat on Dad's left, but I sometimes changed seats and sat by Mom. From one side of the table I could face a view out the window, and from the other side I could see myself in the mirror hanging on our dining room wall. Two extra chairs were always in place, and we could easily add two more plates. People often stopped by, and if we were eating, we always invited them to join us.

Before a meal, Dad would announce, "Let's all pray." My dad didn't grow up in church, so he didn't follow what we would consider to be a traditional practice of "saying grace" before a meal. He didn't pray while we all listened to him; we all said our own prayers at the same time. And because I knew God's presence was at our table, I had too much fear of God and respect for God to come to the table with my rebellious heart and pray. Coming to the table was one thing in my life that helped me make sure my heart was right before God.

It was at the table that I learned to pray out loud. Each person in our family prayed out loud, at the same time—a chorus of spoken prayers together. It was an unusual way to pray at a table, and to this day, I have never witnessed others praying in this way. Our prayers were not memorized, neither were they the same at every meal. Dad wanted to be certain that he could hear all of our mumbled prayers in the background of his. Occasionally, he would ask Mom, Noel, or me to say the prayer, and everyone else waited in silence until the prayer was finished.

At our own family table, my brother and I learned to pray because of my parents' expressions of their grateful hearts. We learned the basic theology of the love and the grace of God from the prayers of our parents while sitting at our table. Our table prayers always included a grateful heart for the goodness of God, for salvation, and for guidance and direction for our lives.

The Family Altar

I believe that the table has the potential to become the family altar. This is not exclusively, of course, because God meets us anywhere we are, at the point of our call to Him. But I have come to believe that there is supernatural presence at work whenever we come to the table. Not only are our bodies nourished and our emotions healed, but our souls are also nurtured at the table. The Bread of the Presence meets us there. All we have to do is fix the food!

> I believe that the table has the potential to become the family altar.

Praying was very important to Mom and Dad. Dad was so grateful for his salvation and newfound peace in his life. We prayed three times a day at our meals and every night before bedtime. The four of us ended our day by going into our living room to pray. Dad knelt at his chair, Mom knelt at another chair, and my brother and I usually knelt at either end of the sofa. This prayer time was different than the way we prayed at the table. During these family prayer times, we could not hear each other. Our prayers were more private. It was our time to talk to God and to ask forgiveness for anything we had done wrong—no one else needed to know. Even when I listened closely, I could not understand what Mom, Dad, or Noel were praying.

When our family had our prayer times in the living room, most of the time I was distracted. I'm not saying that I never prayed during the "family altar," as my parents called it, but most of the time I couldn't concentrate on my prayers. Of course neither Mom nor Dad knew that, because they were busy praying at the other end of the room. My distraction during these prayer times was not out of rebellion or resistance; I was merely fascinated with the colors of the threads in the weave of the sofa fabric. When I was supposed to be praying quietly, I instead found myself counting and creating rows and patterns of colors that could not be seen from a distance. With my head buried in my hands and my eyes merely a few inches from the sofa cushion, I was seeing things that did not otherwise seem to exist. The weave of the fabric became like a kaleidoscope. I gazed into my own world of color, shapes, and texture, completely losing track of what I was supposed to be doing—praying. After fifteen minutes or so—which is a long time to a kid—I could hear Mom or Dad rise from their knees. When their soft-sounding words were quiet, I knew that I could also arise from my kneeling position. Kisses and hugs followed, and away to bed we would go.

We know that prayer is effective and powerful anytime and anywhere we pray (James 5:16). However, in my experience, our table was more of my family's altar than was our sofa. At the table, I could not hide; I had to be respectful and was required to partic-ipate. Later, as a teenager wanting to go my own way and do my own thing, it was easier to pretend to pray while kneeling silently at the sofa than it was to pretend while praying aloud at the table. The presence of God at our table—the Bread of the Presence—soft-ened my heart and brought me to repentance. My independence and early rebellion did not last long. Later, I loved praying at the table and at the sofa. I loved praying while driving the car (with my eyes open!) and at my bedside. Praying at the table took on a whole new meaning. As Jesus invites us all in Revelation 3:20, He knocked, I opened the door, and He came in to dine with me.

Your Table Prayers

However your family decides to pray while at your table, you should choose your own words. Remember, your table prayers don't have to be fancy or elaborate or spoken in King James English (unless that's how you talk!). The words you use should be appropriate for the people and the ages of those who are at your table. For example, if your children are young and you use the term *Redeemer*, you may want to explain to them what that word means. Get your children's input on what they think it means. Table conversation should be a discussion, rather than a lecture. Keep your terms simple, always reinforcing in the lives of your family the hope of salvation and the love of God.

At my family table, when I pray, my prayer may be a version of this: "Jesus, as we gather around our table, we want to thank You for Your presence in our lives. May we never forget that You are our Redeemer and no matter what has happened today, there is no sin that cannot be forgiven. Because of Your love for us, we commit to give You everything. We are grateful to You for our food and for all of Your provision. Thank You. We love You. In Your name we pray. Amen." Anyone who knows my husband, Larry, will know that his table prayer tends to be briefer than mine. Brief prayers are effective too.

Table prayers could be more meaningful if they have a redemptive message, meaning that they include content that remembers an aspect of grace, the hope of salvation, forgiveness, and the love of God because of Christ's sacrifice on the cross. Jesus said that at every meal, we are to intentionally remember the purpose of His broken body and His blood spilled out for our salvation.

I encourage you to examine carefully how you pray at the table and to be more intentional to include hope for your family. In your table prayers, you can include God's love and His willingness to forgive.

> I encourage you to examine carefully how you
> pray at the table and to be more intentional to
> include hope for your family.

For example, if you have young children around your table, you may want to pray something as simple as this: "Jesus, thank You for loving our family and for this time we have together. Help us all feel You close beside us. Thank You that if any of us has done something wrong, You will forgive us if we ask You. Help us always to please You. Thank You for our food, and keep us healthy. In Jesus' name we pray. Amen."

When a non-Christian adult is at your table, you could pray something like this: "Father God, we thank You for Your Son, Jesus Christ, in our lives, and we thank You for the Holy Spirit, who directs our lives to bring You honor. Jesus, I ask that we will all feel Your presence around our table as we share this time with our friends. Let Your joy be among us. Thank You for the power of Your love, and help us to reflect Your love to others. In the name of Jesus we pray. Amen."

When extended family members are sharing a meal with you, your prayer might sound something similar to this: "Jesus, we are so grateful for our family. Extend Your blessing to each person around this table. Help us to always experience Your peace, love, and joy with one another. Thank You that we can come to You with any need and You will redeem our failures. As a family, we seek righteousness in each of our lives. We commit to support and encourage one another. Bless our food and thank You for the one who prepared this meal. In the name of Jesus we pray. Amen."

These simple prayer ideas are to merely stimulate your thinking about the content of your table prayers. Rather than repeating the same thing every time you pray, choose to pray from your heart in a way that those around your table can understand what you are saying.

The table is the place where our bodies are fed, our emotions are healed, and our souls are nourished. Do you feel far from God? Do you want to experience more of God's supernatural power in your life and in the lives of your family members? Then come to the table! When we gather our family around the table, as a family altar, I am convinced that the redemptive presence of Jesus will meet us there in a powerful, supernatural way.

Terrific Table Talk

Build Your Vocabulary

Define a word at your table and talk about the definition. Here are some examples of words you can include in your list:

- redeem
- love
- commit
- transform

Each family member takes a turn using the word in a sentence. Make it funny or teach values merely by the sentences you create.

Table Reflections

1. Why do Jewish and Christian homes still celebrate Passover dinner?

2. What did Jesus demonstrate to his friends when he broke the bread and drank the wine?

3. When Jesus said, "Do this in remembrance of Me" (Luke 22:19), what was He referring to? How often are we to remember this?

4. How can the table become your family altar?

5. Write a simple prayer of redemption for a kindergartner to understand.

Part 3

The Table Is a Place of Participation

Chapter 8

Passing It On

These words, which I am commanding you today, shall be on your heart. You shall teach them diligently to your sons and shall talk of them when you sit in your house and when you walk by the way and when you lie down and when you rise up.

—Deuteronomy 6:6–7

M Y MOTHER IS EIGHTY-SIX years old, and she is very healthy and spry. She rides her stationary bike one hour every day, and she can do more sit-ups than I can. She is full of life and stories. Mom keeps our family heritage alive by linking our generations together with her stories. We love hearing her describe what life was like in the days before electricity, indoor plumbing, telephones, and cars.

One of my favorite stories is the one Mom tells about her parents' spiritual experience. Her mother trusted Jesus on an Oklahoma farm while attending a three-week revival. Ten years later, Grandpa followed her faith. On Sundays, neighbors from nearby farms gathered to hear Grandma talk about the Bible and the significance God's Word was having in her family life. These gatherings eventually moved from house to house in what they called cottage prayer meetings. As the group grew, they moved to the schoolhouse. Later it became a Sunday school and then the first church in their community. Grandma taught the Bible study each Sunday, week after week. My brother and I enjoyed hearing these stories and were well aware of our spiritual heritage.

Mom, the second born of five children, tells how her relationship grew with her mother. Every morning, she would get up early to help Grandma make breakfast. Mom's responsibility was to make the biscuits and set the table. Grandma cooked the meat and the eggs. At times, they also added pancakes or potatoes to the menu. While they cooked breakfast, Mom's older sister made the beds and helped the younger children get dressed for school. Everyone gathered around the table to eat breakfast together. My mother's grandmother, who lived with them, cleaned the kitchen after the kids went to school.

While participating with the meal preparation, Mom bonded with Grandma in a trusting, intimate way. As she became a teenager, it was in the kitchen, early in the mornings, where Mom told Grandma her secrets. She confided in Grandma and felt safe telling her everything—who walked her home from school, who she liked, and who she did not like. Grandma listened, interjecting humor and bits of wisdom. It was natural for them to talk while they worked together in the kitchen.

Practicing God's Commandments

After God gave Moses the Ten Commandments, Moses instructed the children of Israel regarding the importance of teaching their children to practice the commandments in their daily lives.

> *Hear, O Israel! The* LORD *is our God, the* LORD *is one! You shall love the* LORD *your God with all your heart and with all your soul and with all your might. These words, which I am commanding you today, shall be on your heart. You shall teach them diligently to your sons and shall talk of them **when you sit in your house** and when you walk by the way and when you lie down and when you rise up.* (Deut. 6:4–7; emphasis added)

The "words" Moses mentions in this passage are what we know as the Ten Commandments. If I paraphrase this passage to reflect our twenty-first-century lifestyle, Moses is saying that God's commandments will build character in us if we talk about the goodness of God and what pleases Him throughout the day, especially when we come home and *sit in our house.* Where is the place that a family sits in the house and talks face-to-face? It is at the table.

The Ten Commandments are God's values to guide our lives. He tells us what to do and what not to do. If you think about it, the Ten Commandments deal with three very practical relational categories: your relationship with God, your relationship with yourself, and your relationship with others.

Commandments one through three are about our relationship with God:

1. *"You shall have no other gods before me"* (Ex. 20:3). God values commitment.

2. *"You shall not make for yourself an idol"* (Ex. 20:4). God values authenticity.

3. *"You shall not take the name of the Lord your God in vain" (Ex. 20:7).* God values respect.

Commandment four is about our relationship with ourselves:

4. *"Remember the sabbath day, to keep it holy. Six days you shall labor and do all your work, but the seventh day is a sabbath of the Lord your God; in it you shall not do any work" (Ex. 20:8–9).* God values rest.

Commandments five through ten are about our relationships with others:

5. *"Honor your father and your mother" (Ex. 20:12).* God values parents.

6. *"You shall not murder" (Ex. 20:13).* God values life.

7. *"You shall not commit adultery" (Ex. 20:14).* God values marriage.

8. *"You shall not steal" (Ex. 20:15).* God values ownership.

9. *"You shall not bear false witness [lie] against your neighbor"* (Ex. 20:16). God values honesty.

10. *"You shall not covet… anything that belongs to your neighbor" (Ex. 20:17).* God values individuality.

These are the values that are the foundation of good character: faith in God, care for ourselves, and respect for others. These are the kinds of things Mom and Grandma talked about while they made breakfast together. These are the things Mom and I talked about when I helped her make meals for my family. And these are the things Larry and I talked about to our daughter and our son. These principles are now passed on to their children.

> Meaningful, character-strengthening conversation should happen regularly during a lifetime of sharing everyday meals together.

Talking at the table is where most of our meaningful conversation happened. Passing on values and principles, convictions and character, doesn't happen by just eating a few special occasion meals together per year. Meaningful, character-strengthening conversation should happen regularly during a lifetime of sharing everyday meals together.

Conversation Makes a Difference

Recently, National Public Radio's Alix Spiegel explored what the research

Terrific Table Talk

Together with your family, discuss the value words in the Ten Commandments:

1. Commitment
2. Authenticity
3. Respect
4. Rest
5. Parents
6. Life
7. Marriage
8. Ownership
9. Truth
10. Individuality

from the past decade really tells us about the dinner meal in relationship to family outcomes.[1] He was aware of the findings from top American universities, such as Harvard and Purdue, that families who eat meals together do better in every way than those who do not. Their children do better in school, are less likely to be involved in bad habits such as smoking and drinking, and are less likely to experiment with drugs or sex. Alix Spiegel asked Dr. David Dickinson, professor of education at Vanderbilt University, "Is it that dinner itself offers some magical protection, or is there something else at work?"

Professor Dickinson has done his own research on dinner. A number of years ago, he and some researchers from Harvard wanted to figure out why some kids learned to read early while others lagged behind. To do this, they decided to look at family routines. The researchers recorded mealtimes, but they also looked at other things, such as how often parents read to their children and played with their children. According to Dickinson, the group came to the study with some very firm expectations: They fully expected that reading to a child at an early age would have the greatest impact on their literacy. However, he stated, "What we found was that our data on the quality of conversations in mealtimes was a much stronger predictor of how later development would go for children's language and literacy development."[2]

You might think the conclusion of this study to improve literacy in early childhood development would be for families to eat dinner together and read to children early. But as Dickinson will tell you, a deeper look at the study suggests a slightly different conclusion. It turns out that the *content* of the dinner conversations was important. That is, the kids who did well didn't just eat dinner with their families; they ate dinner with families that maintained complex conversation, rich with explanation, storytelling, and discussion.

> Kids who did well didn't just eat dinner with their families; they ate dinner with families that maintained complex conversation, rich with explanation, storytelling, and more.

It's no wonder that the Scripture tells us to talk regularly with our children about God's love, how we relate to others, and how valuable we are to one another.

Character Is Developed at the Table

The table is a place where we can train our children. Although we do not want our mealtimes to have a rigid classroom environment, conversation at the table can develop character and learning ability through natural, positive interaction.

Dinnertime is a great opportunity to encourage and build up one another. This is done with affirming comments to the stories others are telling as well as compliments for their behavior, their participation, and their courtesies. Praise your children when they use good manners. This is a way to reinforce good behavior without constantly correcting them for poor behavior. Saying things like, "I like the way you are sitting so tall" to one child can cause another child who is slumped to sit up straight. Sometimes, straightening your own posture without saying a word will motivate others to sit up straight. Everyone feels better about themselves in a positive environment.

> Dinnertime is a great opportunity to encourage and build up one another.

Good manners are simply rules of kindness and consideration for others. Talking with your mouth full is not courteous to those who have to look at you. Chewing with your mouth closed helps prevent you from choking. When a person understands the good reason behind an instruction, it is easier to want to apply an improved behavior. When food is passed around the table family style, family members learn to share. They take just enough for themselves so there is plenty for others. Taking your turn to talk and not interrupting shows respect for others. Remaining at the table until everyone is finished and has been excused reinforces patience and respect. These are just a few examples to show how character is built during the dinner experience.

Psalm 128 describes some of the many blessings of those who fear the Lord and walk in His ways. In verse 3, the Psalmist says, "Your children [will be] like olive plants around your table." Why did David say that our children will be like olive trees *around our tables*? I think it is because olive trees can stand strong for centuries; no storm in life can topple a mature olive tree because its roots go so deep. In fact, when I was visiting the Garden of Gethsemane in Israel several years ago, I saw olive trees that have been there for hundreds of years.

So it is with those who have strong character. There is no storm in life that children who grow up around the table with the Bread of the Presence and grace-filled positive conversation cannot endure. When they become adults, no matter how tough some experiences can seem, those experiences will not uproot them. They will have deep roots and the character to endure.

In Matthew 13:1–23, Jesus told a story to demonstrate the importance of our character. In this story, there is a sower, some seed, and various types of soil. The sower is Jesus, the seed is His principles, and the soil is the hearts of people. He said that when the seed (the principles He had been teaching) is sown on rocky soil, it does not go deep because the soil is shallow. Although this person is excited about the new truths from the Word he is learning, when he encounters a storm in life, the principles he knows wither away and he falls back into his old habit patterns. Jesus explains that the person falls away because "He has no firm root in himself" (v. 21). In other words, this person has no depth of character.

This is why it is essential to build good character in our lives and in our families. So when we hear the Word of God, we can grasp it, understand it, and God's principles will grow from the depth of our character and shape our hearts. We will not be uprooted by a temptation or a trial, because our roots run deep with strong character.

Shape Character With Good Conversation

One way to encourage conversation at your family table is to select a theme to discuss for each meal. For example:

- Monday: Talk about food—its origin, how it is grown, its nutritious value.

- Tuesday: Bring a cartoon to the table and think of creative captions.

- Wednesday: Talk about the day.

- Thursday: What famous person would you like to bring to dinner, and why?

- Friday: Play "finish the sentence." If you treat the family to a restaurant meal, this is a great conversation starter in a public place. It is a good time to practice manners in public.

- Saturday: Find a topic in a current newspaper or magazine and bring it to the table for discussion.

- Sunday: Discuss one of the topics from that week's sermon or Sunday school lesson during Sunday dinner. This is a great time to share a meal with someone else. Bring a family home with you after church. This might be the time to have a kids' table near the adult table and give them a break from you and let them enjoy their friends.

Mom Shaped My Character through Participation

When I was growing up, my mother used to quote this verse to me: "The wise woman builds her house, but the foolish tears it down with her own hands" (Prov. 14:1). This proverb explains the importance of wisdom in shaping the lives of those who are in our homes.

My mother is truly a wise woman. Mom tells the story of the time she heard what she believed to be the voice of the Lord say to her, *If you were not here, have you given Devi everything she needs to be an effective manager of her home?* I was only twelve years old. Mom actually thought this was a warning that she may not live long. Taking this impression seriously, she began requiring my participation with her in all of our household duties. She did not make me do them on my own. She showed me how, and I worked by her side. Mom was training me for my future.

When she cooked, I cooked with her. For a season, she baked pies daily for a local restaurant. No one can bake a pie like my mother, but after learning from her, I come in with a close second. She would say, "Now Devi, to seal the top crust to the bottom crust, you should dampen it with water. Here, just wet your finger and run it around the edge." Then I would follow her lead. She continued to tell me to set the oven at 400 degrees for fifteen minutes because this will cook the bottom crust, and then turn the oven down to 350 degrees to complete the baking. She always told me what to do and why I was to do it that way. She showed me and then she allowed me to do it on my own, praising me for my attempt.

When it was time to set the table, Mom would tell me to use the prettiest dishes. I could choose which ones I wanted for that meal. This gave room for my own creativity and decision-making. When the table was set, I had a great sense of accomplishment! We played games and sang songs while we worked. Seldom was I sent off to work alone.

My mom helped my grandmother, I helped my mother, my daughter helped me, and her daughters helped her. Now, Sophia, my great-granddaughter, is helping her mother at 2 years old. Our son's daughters also help their mother. The blessings of the generations are passed on. God told Moses to choose life so that you may live, you and your descendants, by loving the Lord your God, obeying His voice and by holding fast to Him (Deut. 30:19–20).

In our family, this blessings-of-the-generations began being passed on while Mom made biscuits with Grandma early in the morning.

A Place to Build Up, Not to Tear Down

It is not just eating at the table that makes a difference; it is eating at the table with the presence of grace that matters. Grace that sees beyond spilled milk. My mother's comment when we spilled our milk always was, "Don't cry over spilled milk." She added, "Just clean it up." Mom was teaching a life lesson to us during a time that we could have been scolded and shamed. Instead of yelling at us and being impatient with us when we made a mess, whether it was the result of carelessness or an accident, she taught us to make the best out of the situation and move on. She taught us that we could not change what just happened, but we could attempt to make it right by cleaning up the mess we made. This simple instruction shaped our character.

> It is not just eating at the table that makes a difference; it is eating at the table with the presence of grace that matters.

It is very detrimental to the human heart to make a person feel ashamed. "What did you do?" "Why did you do that?" "I can't believe you just did that. I told you to be careful!" These kinds of statements cause a person to feel value-less. Instead, the Bible tells us that our words are always to be with grace, which is favor that is undeserved (Col. 4:6). We are to demonstrate grace to others throughout the meal, not just to "say grace" before a meal. When someone says something inappropriate at the table—give grace. When your child's behavior is out of order—give grace.

Sometimes when we are rushed, when the day has been challenging and hectic and sitting at a peaceful meal seems impossible, it helps me to enter the kitchen and light a candle. The serenity of the flickering flame and the soothing fragrance of the candle help me to calm down. Perhaps there have been impatient, harsh words spoken and there is tension between family members. This is not the time to cancel supper plans and go to the drive through. This is the time to set the table, even if you bring in takeout food or order pizza to be delivered. This gives you time to renew your heart, create an atmosphere that restores the harsh words, and replace any unkind words with words of encouragement. A humble confession of "I'm sorry for being such a grump" can begin to bring redemption to the hearts of your family at the table and will give them courage to apologize when they are wrong.

When Food Isn't Fun—Disobedience at the Table

What do we do when our children disobey at the table? What about those times when they really do need correction or discipline? The type of disobedience and unrest at the table created by children is varied depending on their ages. Let me say, if you are just implementing these new values for older children who have not yet learned to sit properly and interact considerately at the table, they will not change overnight. Your table time will likely be less peaceful in the beginning than it will become later. The key is to be consistent and to make your time together at the table as fun as possible. Try not to be rigid. This is not a time for everyone to sit still and be quiet. It is a time for your family members to talk and to take turns.

Should there be a disobedience that requires instruction and correction, tell your child that you will take care of the situation after dinner is over. You must not forget to keep your promise to address their conduct after dinner! Let them know that their interruption of your family time around the table will not give them permission to be dismissed; neither will it prevent the rest of the family from having a good time together.

I never remember being sent from the table during dinner. And Larry and I did not ever send our children away from the table when they misbehaved. Instead, we promised them that after dinner we will discuss what happened—whether it was an unkind word from Trina to her brother or a kick under the table from Aaron to Trina. And we never forgot our promise.

If a young child is extremely belligerent, throwing a defiant screaming fit at the table, you should remove the child from the table, take him or her to a private place in the home, and deal with the problem. Then both of you should return to the table. Whatever you do, do not send your child to his or her bedroom and use leaving the meal as their punishment. You want the table to be a place that your children do not associate with punishment. Your table should always be viewed as a happy place of interaction, warmth, and acceptance.

> Your table should always be viewed as a happy place of interaction, warmth, and acceptance.

Conversation Starters

When you sit at your table, your family's conversation can be like art. You begin with a blank canvas, and one brush stroke leads to another stroke. Sometimes the artist knows what he wants the painting to be and other times it evolves to something not expected. Good conversation skills can be learned, yet few of us really have those skills. Yes, some people are naturally outgoing and talkative, but that does not mean that they know how to get others to converse with them. Talking at the table can be a great way to reach deep into another person's thoughts, experiences, and opinions, or merely to share the events of the day. What we do not want to do at the table is legislate and control every minute of the table talk, preventing spontaneity. In some ways it can be a balancing act. Like the artist painting the canvas, some strokes are detailed and precise with concentrated color; others are random and freehanded, creating a blend of pastels.

Good conversation skills are important in all aspects of our daily experiences. Recently, a couple went to dinner with her husband's boss and his wife. She had casually met him but did not know his wife. Knowing that both families held Christian values, soon after they sat down and placed their dinner order, she asked, "So tell me your salvation story." Wow! What a conversation starter. The conversation revealed their lifestyle before committing their lives to Christ, the surrounding events that brought them to Christ, and their deep gratitude for their daily walk with Him and His blessing in their business. The conversation was not awkward; it was edifying and they left knowing each other in a deeper way than they would have if there had not been a purposeful question asked.

I have created a list of recommended conversation starters to get you thinking about creative ways you can discreetly interject conversation that creates interesting responses around your table. Do not announce what you are doing; just ask an interesting question and see what evolves. Try another question later if the people around the table still seem disconnected. Be sure to do this in a way that does not seem contrived. Be intentional about helping your children or friends to develop their conversation skills.

Try some of the conversation starters below, and then create your own. Just remember that this is not a time to teach; it is a time to talk. Make your questions age-appropriate to those who will be eating at your table. You may ask your children to compose one question for the family and let then take the lead in the conversation. It could be amazing the kind of picture they create on your table conversation canvas.

1. What is your biggest dream?
2. What is your biggest fear?
3. What does being popular mean to you?
4. What makes you smile?
5. What mistake has taught you the biggest lesson?
6. What has been the happiest day of your life?
7. What do you think heaven will be like?
8. How would you define *rich*?
9. How would you feel if someone surprised you with a party?
10. How do you like to spend your free time?
11. How has God shown you His love?
12. Tell about your favorite teacher.

13. Tell a story about a grandparent.
14. Tell about your salvation experience.
15. Tell a favorite church memory.
16. Define *success*.
17. Describe a time when you were brave.
18. Describe God.
19. What is the first thing you would do if you were given a thousand dollars?
20. If you could rename yourself, what name would you choose?

Pass the Blessings, Please!

Deuteronomy 7:9 says, "Know therefore that the LORD your God, He is God, the faithful God, who keeps His covenant and His lovingkindness to a thousandth generation with those who love Him and keep His commandments." It is awesome to know that God has promised that He will pass his blessings on to our next generation.

You may be a first-generation Christian in your family. If this is the case, you have the opportunity to create new family practices and traditions that will encourage the next generation to participate with you as you love God with all of your heart. Your love for Him will be passed on.

> God has promised that He will pass his blessings on to our next generation.

You may be like me and have the privilege of walking in the truth and godly character that has been passed to you from previous generations who have loved God with all of their hearts and have trained you in His ways. I do not want to be the generation that does not pass the blessing on because of my careless living. By setting the table and talking (not preaching) of God's ways when we get up in the morning, eat breakfast, go to work or school, come home, do homework, prepare dinner, and watch television, we will surely have the blessings of God and our next generations will be blessed with His loving-kindness as promised. This is what my parents did, and their actions made God real to me. As God's love was demonstrated to me every day, I participated in His ways along with Mom and Dad. His ways became my ways. And they can become the ways of your family too.

Table Reflections

1. List several values that you want to intentionally pass on to your children.

2. Create a practical way to discuss these values. Keep it natural.

3. According to research, what was the strongest predictor of good literacy development in children?

4. List three character traits that can be developed while eating meals at the table.

5. Define *grace* and illustrate how grace can be experienced at the table.

Chapter 9
Renewed Relationships

Let us eat and celebrate; for this son of mine was dead and has come to life again; he was lost and has been found.

—Luke 15:23–24

I SAT ON THE LIVING room floor about six feet from the television watching our local version of *American Bandstand,* known as *Record Hop*. Each Tuesday night, the popular dance show opened with local high school cheerleaders leading their team cheer. The dancing crowd included students from that school. That night, my high school was in the spotlight. Our cheerleaders and pom-pom girls, dressed in their black, orange, and white uniforms, marched into their places to the beat of the drum corps. Their routines were synchronized, and I knew every step, every kick, and every twirl. I knew every girl's name. I watched as if I was there. Tears were streaming down my face because I wanted to be there so badly. I knew their routines had to be adjusted because one girl was missing. I was that girl.

My parents did not allow me to attend school dances; therefore, I was not allowed to participate in the cheerleading performance on this live dance program. They were sincere in guarding my activities and choices, but at the age of fourteen, I did not fully appreciate their love and protection of me. In the ensuing months, I made some decisions without my parents' knowledge because I did not think that my old-fashioned parents knew much about the youth of my generation.

Secretly, I devised plans to attend dances and to do other things that my parents would not have approved of. I vividly remember the night I planned to sneak out of my bedroom so I could go with some older kids I hardly knew into the nearby city and drag Main Street. A friend's older brother and his friend were home from college, and they were going to drive us around that night. My friends had invited me to drag Main Street many times, but most of them knew that I was not allowed to go, so they went without me. Finally, this time, I was going to go.

Everything was arranged. My friends and I agreed that if my bedroom light was on, it would be a sign that it was not safe for me to sneak out of the window because Mom and Dad were not yet asleep. If my light was off when they drove up, that was a sign for my friends to wait in the car while I climbed out the window, because my Mom and Dad were fast asleep.

At school that day, I was so excited to finally have this experience. My friends and I talked about it, planned, and strategized. I had both butterflies and knots in my stomach—butterflies from excitement and knots from fear and guilt. My heart was conflicted. I wanted to have fun, but I did not want to do wrong. I knew I couldn't do both.

Mom had dinner ready as usual that evening. I didn't feel like eating, but she insisted that I come to the table. I was quiet at dinner, and Dad asked me if I was okay. I assured him that I was fine but just didn't feel well. I remember thinking how terrific my parents were and how much I loved them. I knew if they found out what I was planning, they would be so hurt. Deep inside, I did not want to hurt them.

I'm not sure what our dinner conversation was about that night. I do know that my brother was a senior and played all of the sports. Dad was an avid sports fan, so often our table talk revolved around Noel's sports in his final year of high school. It was not unusual for football players to eat dinner at our house before a game, and we always attended his games, no matter where they were played, on our home field or away. This year, I cheered for my brother's games. I was really proud to be his sister, and I did not want him to be disappointed in me either.

At the table that night, I felt like two people—the baby sister of the big brother I adored and the wild-at-heart teenager who wanted to have fun. How could I be both? Would I sneak out the window at 11 p.m. to return at 2 a.m. or would I stay home? It's no wonder I was not hungry. That was a lot for a young girl to decide!

As planned, my parents went to bed at their usual time and were sound asleep. I went to my bedroom and pretended to go to bed. After I knew they were asleep, I got up, dressed, and proceeded with my plan. With my bedroom light off, at 10:55 p.m., I stood at my window watching for the car to drive up on the road beside our white picket fence. Purse in hand, I was ready for my first fun night out! I saw headlights coming from a distance and make the turn to come close to the fence. I froze. I thought, *I can't do this. My mom and dad love me too much. I cannot do this to them. What will they think of me if I get caught?* My heart was racing. The car outside quietly idled while waiting for me. The plan was working except for one thing that I had not expected: I remembered dinner.

The laughter around our family dinner table that night, the loving glances, the plans for the next day all rushed through my mind. *After tonight, what will dinners be like for me?* I wondered. I didn't have answers; I just knew that I could not do this. I walked to the door of my bedroom instead of to my already cracked window, and I turned the light switch on. To my friends, this meant it was not safe for me to sneak out. They drove away.

My life could have gone a very different direction with lifelong consequences that night. What if I had not been with my family at the table for dinner? Turning on the light switch was one of the most important decisions I have ever made. Cooking dinner that night was Mom's important decision.

That was the last temptation of that dimension that I had through my high school years. Soon after, I committed my life to Christ and began to make decisions that would please Him and my parents. My internal relationship was renewed with my family at the table. That night at the table, the conflict within me began to be resolved. And by the way, years later, my parents told me that they regretted not allowing me to go to the live dance show with my cheerleading team. I had already forgiven them.

A Place of Restoration

There is no life experience that replaces the connection and significance created by eating together at the table. Whether young or old, when a person experiences trauma, temptation, or embarrassment, being invited to the table makes them feel valued and restores their sense of significance.

There is no life experience that replaces the connection and significance created by eating together at the table.

Have you ever found yourself doing the unthinkable? While feeling trapped in an unexpected circumstance, you told a lie you did not plan to tell or said things you regret. You reacted outside of your personal values and who you really are. It is an awesome awareness to know that no matter what you encounter during a day—an intense argument with an employee, a misunderstanding with your spouse, or an impatient outburst with your children—there is grace at your table when you join your family for dinner. Although you may have already prayed and repented while driving home, when you sit at your table, just knowing that the Bread of the Presence will restore your embarrassment and regret for your lack of self-control brings amazing relief. The love and affirmation from your family members will give you courage to face tomorrow with dignity.

Let me share three biblical examples of people whose relationships were restored while sharing a meal.

Peter

On the night Jesus was arrested, the apostle Peter did the unthinkable! When a young servant girl pointed out that Peter was one of the men with Jesus, Peter denied that he even knew Jesus. He said to her, "I do not know what you are talking about" (Matt. 26:69–70). This happened three times, and each time someone identified Peter as a friend of Jesus, Peter strongly disagreed. When someone said, "Surely you too are one of them; for even the way you talk gives you away," Peter was so angry that he cursed at them and belligerently lied again (vv. 72–74). At that moment, a rooster crowed and Peter remembered the words of Jesus. He "went out and wept bitterly," overcome with shame that he had denied his Savior and Lord (v. 75).

But thankfully, the story doesn't end there. John 21 tells about how Jesus appeared to Peter and restored their relationship during a shared meal. After the crucifixion of Jesus, Peter returned to Galilee and was on a boat fishing when he and his friends heard a man calling from the shore, asking if they had caught any fish yet. They replied that they had been fishing all night, but their nets were empty. The man on the shore told them to cast their nets on the other side of the boat, and their nets would be full.

Immediately Peter and his friends recognized that the man calling to them from the shore was none other than their Lord, who had died on the cross, was buried in a tomb, and was now alive again! When Peter recognized Jesus' voice calling from the shore, he was so enthused to see Jesus that he jumped into the water and swam to shore while the others brought the boat to dock.

What was Jesus doing on the shore while He was waiting for them to dock the boat? He was cooking breakfast—fish and bread (John 21:9). In His final days on earth, Jesus gave Peter, who must have been overwhelmed with shame, an opportunity to talk to Him while breaking bread together. After they ate breakfast, Jesus asked Peter if he loved Him. I can't even imagine how Peter must have felt. He had done the unthinkable and was caught! Here he was, face-to-face with a loving friend who searched him out and cooked breakfast for him so they could have a very important conversation.

Jesus very carefully chose the right questions, which caused Peter to talk openly. He simply asked Peter, "Do you love me?" This gave Peter an opportunity to restate what was in his heart. What grace Jesus showed by cooking breakfast and talking to Peter!

> In His final days on earth, Jesus gave Peter, who must have been overwhelmed with shame, an opportunity to talk to Him while breaking bread together.

Notice that Jesus did not address the issue of Peter's failure, nor did He try to make Peter feel badly for what he had done. Jesus did not interrogate Peter, asking him a series of questions about why he had lied. And more importantly, Jesus did not remind Peter that He had been right all along. After all, at the Last Supper Jesus had warned Peter that he would deny Him (Matt. 26:34), so He could have said, "See, I told you so!"

Being together, face-to-face, and sharing a meal can take away the blame and shame of having done something that we deeply regret. Jesus gave Peter favor that he did not deserve by cooking breakfast for him. This truly is amazing grace.

King David

King David is another biblical example of someone who was restored at the table. As we saw in chapter 6, King David talks about his relationship with the Good Shepherd in Psalm 23. In the first three verses of this psalm, he recalls what the Good Shepherd has done in his life, and he identifies four elements that God used to shape his character:

- *"He makes me" (v. 2)*—God disciplined David.
- *"He leads me" (v. 2)*—God was the standard and the example for David to follow.
- *"He restores me" (v. 3)*—God affirmed David and always gave him another opportunity.
- *"He guides me" (v. 3)*—God taught David His principles.

These interactions of discipline, example, affirmation, and instruction guided David to become a great leader in God's kingdom. In the same way God's heart was to restore David, God's heart is to restore all of us when we fail.

In verse 5, David says, "You prepare a table before me in the presence of my enemies; You have anointed my head with oil; my cup overflows." Because the actions in this verse are punctuated with semicolons and not periods, I am making an assumption that when the Shepherd prepared a table for David in the presence of his enemies and anointed his head with oil, God anointed David while he was *at the table*! David was restored from his shame of failure and affirmed by God at the table, and God empowered David to face the enemy with God's anointing. This gave David a new confidence; he was restored and felt stronger and more capable than he had ever felt. Plus, his cup of joy was overflowing with his newfound security and identity, not in himself and his own abilities but in the person the Shepherd was shaping him to become.

David concludes, "Surely goodness and lovingkindness will follow me all the days of my life, and I will dwell in the house of the LORD forever" (v. 6). Because of his relationship with the Good Shepherd, David was restored in the presence of his enemies, and he became a sensitive man with strong character, deep passion, and spiritual desire.

I believe that Psalm 23 is a great guide for parenting, leadership training, and character development. This psalm presents characteristics that are necessary to mold character and cultivate spiritual desire in those we lead. These principles establish the potential for restoration that can take place in a person's heart when we prepare our table for them. Their hearts and lives will once again overflow with joy and fulfillment, giving them a new destiny.

Jehoiachin

In 2 Kings 24:8, we learn of a teenage king of Judah named Jehoiachin, who also experienced restoration at the table. After only a three-month reign, this young king suffered a devastating defeat, surrendered to King Nebuchadnezzar, and was taken captive to Babylon. For nearly four decades, Jehoiachin languished in prison in Babylon.

Jehoiachin had done evil in his brief reign as king of Judah, and God allowed Nebuchadnezzar to overthrow Judah and imprison Jehoiachin for decades. Thirty-seven years later, there was a new king of Babylon, and he released Jehoiachin from prison. "So Jehoiachin put aside his prison clothes and for the rest of his life ate regularly at the king's table" (2 Kings 25:29). Jehoiachin's honor and dignity were restored when he was included at the king's table. The king's sincere act of restoring Jehoiachin and bringing him to his table gave Jehoiachin an opportunity to experience God's grace and forgiveness and gave him value in the king's eyes.

This biblical story reminds me of the day Larry was going to pick up a young man from prison who had been incarcerated for thirteen years for assault and rape. He would be taking off his prison clothes that day, and Larry and I had agreed to have him in our home as a guest for a few months as he transitioned to life outside the prison walls.

The morning our new resident was scheduled to arrive, I thought, *What would a man who has spent the past thirteen years in prison want to eat for dinner?* I took a pot roast from the freezer and put it in the oven. Then I quickly baked two apple pies. I set the table routinely and went about my busy day. Soon after I arrived home that afternoon, I finished the preparations and called the family to dinner. Only our son lived with us at the time because by then, his sister was married. We ate in the dining room because our kitchen was too small for a table to seat four. I called the guys to dinner, and when we entered the dining room, I'll never forget what happened.

My husband, Larry, was seated and so was our son, Aaron. I graciously showed our new resident the place where he was to sit. He approached the chair and then stopped. He just stood there as if his feet were stuck to the floor. I encouraged him to be seated because the food was already placed on the table and we were ready to eat. The pot roast and gravy were steaming, and so were the potatoes and carrots. Again, I kindly asked him to have a seat. He looked at me as if he did not hear me. His face was blank, but I noticed that his chin was quivering. He said, "Devi, I have never sat at a table like this before." What he meant was that he had never had dinner at home with his family or any other family. Never had he been invited to a prepared table, set with a tablecloth, matching plates, and properly placed silverware.

I cannot think but that this man's life could have gone a different direction if the dinner experience had been part of his daily routine. He had committed a violent act of force with a woman he did not know. It's beyond me to fully comprehend the extreme desperation one must feel to force himself on another person, seeking to fulfill his own desires. Could it be a distorted, sordid way of seeking to satisfy his essential need for connection and love, if only for a moment? Perhaps this young man's life would have been very different had his mom or dad merely set the table for their meals and eaten together. While this former prisoner lived with us, his favorite time of the day was our dinnertime, when we talked, we laughed, and we loved.

A Place of Resolution

In Luke 15:11–32, Jesus tells the parable of the prodigal son. This son had been given his entire inheritance by his loving father, and then he went to a distant land and squandered it all on wild living.

One day, while working in the fields, his father looked up and saw his wayward son approaching from afar, shuffling down the dusty road. The boy was worn, disheveled, weary, and hungry, but he was finally returning home, ashamed of what he had done. His father was elated at his son's return. As they embraced, the boy expressed his humiliation and repentance. How did his father respond? By throwing a feast and inviting everyone to dine at the table in honor of his restored son! With overwhelming joy and exuberance, and without any blame or accusation for what his son had done in the past, his father welcomed him home and celebrated the present. Did his father know what the future held? No. But his embrace and full inclusion of his son back into the family fold gave the boy hope for a better future, with wisdom gained by his personal experience.

We do not know the details of the daily relationship between this father and his rebellious younger son, but we can imagine what it could have been because of our real-life experiences. I know numerous family stories between fathers and sons, mothers and daughters who experienced a cavernous breach in their relationships during a season of their children's rebellion and destructive choices. Angry hurtful words were spoken to one another that could never be retrieved. No amount of argument, accusations, and threats could persuade either party to understand and concede. Their children turned to living their newly defined morality and lifestyles sometimes ending in destructive addictions, which created homelessness. These mothers and fathers have spent endless nights praying and weeping for their children.

This could have been the plight of the father of the prodigal who spent all the money his father had set aside for him to help make his life successful. But instead of waiting to receive his inheritance at the proper time, the prodigal son did his own thing—and his own thing took him to the bottom, to the place where pigs lived.

The best part of the story is that the son eventually came home. What a picture of love when the father called for a celebration! I'm sure that at the feast, their table conversation did not rehearse past disputes or emphasize how right the father had been. Instead, their interaction at the table must have been filled with gratitude and gratefulness that the family was together and the son was safe and alive. What a time to rejoice! Nothing else matters at this point of resolution.

When we prepare a dinner for our children who have made destructive choices, we let them know beyond a doubt that they are forgiven and restored. The table is the best place to express that love and forgiveness. When they come home, set the table for them. Create an environment at the table for them to talk. Listen to them freely, and restore them fully. You have probably already said everything that there is to say about their poor choices. Let it go. Just invite them over for dinner and dress the table to their liking, and then add a little more so they feel really special. Let your conversation be full of grace and allow the Bread of the Presence to do His work to resolve the issues that were once a point of division. Agreement is not necessary. Enjoy the bonding and unified hearts of love as you eat your meal.

When we prepare a dinner for our children who have made destructive choices, we let them know beyond a doubt that they are forgiven and restored.

A Place of Reconciliation

A few years ago, my daughter's husband announced to her and their four children that he had filed for divorce and was moving out of their home. They had been married for eighteen years. He didn't give much explanation. Every family member was in shock, fearful of a future without the man they each loved so deeply. The painful process of his leaving and removing personal items from their home to a nearby apartment seemed more than any of them could bear.

On the surface, their family life was great—they appeared to be a model Christian family. Dad was a hard worker and worked long hours building a successful business. Mom and the children remained committed to school, church, and extracurricular activities. However, in the midst of the apparent normalcy of their family life, their home was slowly and silently being torn apart. Almost imperceptibly, a tiny fissure had been opened in the sanctity of their home. One of the first areas my son-in-law began to overlook was his participation at the family table. Building his business became more important than being home for dinner with his family. When he was able to join the family at dinner or other meals, his presence became more distant and not quite as heartfelt.

Soon, there was an empty plate at the head of the table.

For whatever reason he was pulled away from that plate, chaos began its course. That tiny crack in the family grew and eventually affected everyone, stifling their togetherness, peace, and tranquility and smothering their joy. It festered. It grew. It worked its destruction.

Trina and our grandchildren prayed together daily that he would come to his senses and return home. He was emotionally shut down but obviously experiencing deep inner turmoil. After he had been out of the home for a little while, he apparently began to realize that his time together with his family at the table was something he missed tremendously. He began stopping by the house after work to see the children, and they would invite him to stay for dinner.

Incredulous friends asked my daughter, "After what your husband did to you and the children, how can you let him come and have dinner with you and the kids every evening?" My daughter replied, "I would allow a stranger to sit at my table. And I would also allow an enemy to sit at my table. Right now, he is both."

Every time he sat down at the dinner table with his family, he would talk. At the next meal, he would talk a little more. In time, he revealed the reason for his abrupt desertion of his wife and children and the disruption of his family. It was at the table while dining in a restaurant with his wife that he finally confessed his sin. He explained that he had become fond of another woman, that he had been living a lie, and that he felt he had to move out. Long work hours, coupled with time on the road and away from his family, had opened a tiny fissure that grew and widened until the heat of his illicit passion burned through the precious fabric of his family.

It was at the table that he received forgiveness. It was the connection with his family and the power of the Bread of the Presence at their table that drew my son-in-law back to his home. Humbled and repentant, he admitted his neglect of his family and his duties as a Christian man, husband, and father. He returned to them with a resolve and determination to rebuild anew, in order to prevent such behavior in the future. And they forgave him.

A few months later, their marriage was restored, and the family regained their strength, happiness, and vitality. Now their time together around the family table is more significant than ever before. Because of this complete restoration, they now enjoy their grandchildren, along with their four children and their spouses and soon-to-be spouses. They are a deeply connected, happy family when they gather around the table. They have experienced the true power of redemption and reconciliation.

I Need To

A few years ago, I was invited to participate in a Spring Fling hosted by the women's ministry of a large church. The church auditorium was filled with women attending Friday evening and two sessions on Saturday morning. I was their guest speaker for this grand event, and their theme was selected from the title of my book *The Home Experience: Making Your Home a Sanctuary of Love and a Haven of Peace*. I spoke on the convincing message of the table principle, and hundreds of women responded to make a commitment to prioritize their daily schedules to include eating meals together with their families at the dinner table.

On Saturday morning, while I was being escorted to the green room to enter the stage and bring the second message of the weekend, I was stopped in the hallway by a lovely lady who asked if she could tell me her story. She promised to be brief, so I listened with intent.

She was a single mom with two children, a teenage daughter and an older son who had been "somewhat of a prodigal," she said. That week, her son had made the decision to come home. Their apartment was small, and in her son's absence, she and her daughter did not bother to get a table. They ate holding a plate on their laps in front of the television. But on her son's return, she began feeling that they should have a table. This nagging feeling led her to go to a discount store and buy an inexpensive table with four chairs so they could sit together for their meals. She purchased the table the day before she heard my message.

While her nineteen-year-old son was assembling the table, he received a phone call from his friend, inviting him to go out with them that evening. He declined. His friend pleaded with him to come. He resisted. His mother heard him tell his friend what he was doing: "I'm putting together a table that my mother just purchased

165

for our apartment." His friend asked, "Why?" He firmly replied, "Because I need to!"

This mother shared with me that her son instinctively felt he needed to participate in making it possible for their family to have a table for the first time. The three of them ate together that evening. It was their first dinner experience together at a table in their home.

Her son's table manners were not very good, and neither were his sister's. But their mom decided that when her daughter tilted the chair on it back legs, rather than telling her what not to do, she would keep the table experience positive, giving suggestions of what to do. She told her that if she kept her chair straight, it would last longer and not break the legs of the chair. Her daughter readily accepted her encouragement without defensiveness because she was proud of their new table and chair set.

The day after her family sat at their new table, she attended the women's conference and heard me speak on the table principle. At that moment, she understood that something supernatural was transpiring in each of their hearts. Potential was being revealed in each one of them—the potential to love, forgive, and embrace one another.

Table Reflections

1. How do you think Peter felt after he denied knowing Jesus and being one of his followers?

2. What did Jesus do to make Peter feel valued once again?

3. When David was filled with fear because of the oppression of his enemies, what did the Good Shepherd do to calm his fear?

4. How was David's life transformed by being seated at the table?

5. Who has become a stranger and an enemy in your relationships? What steps do you need to take to restore that relationship?

Chapter 10

The Extra Plate

For who is greater, the one who is at the table or the one who serves?
Is it not the one who is at the table? But I am among you as one
who serves.

—Luke 22:27

CHUALAR, A CENTRAL CALIFORNIA town just ten miles south of Salinas on Highway 101, was home for me from birth until I married in 1964. When I was seven, our family purchased a well-maintained home on the corner at the edge of town. Our front yard fence bordered the shoulder of the two-lane frontage road to the freeway. On the other side of the freeway was a railroad track. The hobos, as we called them, rode the train and would get off in our small town. Because our house was close to the road, it was the first home they would approach to ask for food.

I vividly remember one night when a hobo was sitting at our dining room table eating a meal. He was dirty and very smelly. Mom made him a sandwich and a warm bowl of soup, and she seated him at our table.

Just outside the back door, where our guests usually entered, sat a wooden picnic table. If I was home alone and a stranger came to our door asking for food, I had been instructed by my parents to seat him at the picnic table and then go inside, make a sandwich, and take it out to him. Dad literally believed Hebrews 13:2: "Do not neglect to show hospitality to strangers, for by this some have entertained angels without knowing it." My parents demonstrated compassion and generosity, and this attitude of kindness and hospitality was naturally developed into the fabric of our daily routines. We were taught not to judge a person on the outside—after all, he or she may be an angel—so we were taught to include everyone in our lives. If people were hungry, we seated them at our table and fed them. My parents demonstrated love to everyone, even to those who were outcasts and homeless, and their example of hospitality had a tremendous influence on my brother and me.

Not only did we feed the strangers who came to our door, but also I vividly remember Dad bringing to our table the town drunk and sobering him up with hot coffee, then driving him home to his family. He was our friend and I went to school with his children. These acts of kindness were normal in our family. And this way of life remains normal to me.

The extra plate always set at our family's dinner table exemplifies a central part of God's character. Extending hospitality to others demonstrates the generosity of God's love.

Extending hospitality to others demonstrates
the generosity of God's love.

Making Strangers Friends

In the Bible, God reminds us of the importance of practicing hospitality. Romans 12:13 commands us to "Share with God's people who are in need. Practice hospitality." In 1 Peter 4:9, we are told, "Offer hospitality to one another without grumbling." And in 3 John 1:8, the apostle concludes, "We ought therefore to show hospitality to such men so that we may work together for the truth."

The Greek word *philoxenos* is translated to the English word *hospitality*. The Greek definition is divided into two parts: *philo* means "friend" and *xenos* means "stranger." *Hospitality* literally means "making strangers friends." Stranger does not necessarily mean only a strange person that you have never met before but it means that hospitality overcomes the distance of strangeness and the tension of being different.[1]

> *Hospitality* literally means "making strangers friends."

While Jesus was teaching His disciples, recorded in Luke 10: 25–29, He was challenged by an educated lawyer who asked Him, "Teacher, what shall I do to inherit eternal life?" Jesus answered by referring to the Law, which this man had spent his entire life studying: "What is written in the Law? How does it read to you?" The quick-witted lawyer had a ready answer, quoting Deuteronomy 6:5: "You shall love the Lord your God with all your heart, and with all your soul, and with all your strength, and with all your mind; and your neighbor as yourself." Jesus responded, "You have answered correctly; do this and you will live."

Then the lawyer defensively asked, "And who is my neighbor?" Jesus replied by telling him a story we know as the parable of the good Samaritan. In this story, a man was traveling on the road from Jerusalem to Jericho when he fell among robbers who stripped him, beat him, and left him half dead. Three different types of people passed by this beaten man: a priest who walked on the other side of the road, perhaps pretending not to see him; a Levite who also passed him on the other side of the road; and a Samaritan, a lowly commoner, who felt compassion and took the injured man to an inn and took care of him and paid for his room and his continued care until he recovered.

Jesus then asked the lawyer, "Which of these three do you think proved to be a neighbor to the man who fell into the robbers' hands?" The lawyer realized that the answer to his original question, "What must I do to inherit eternal life?" was "Show mercy and hospitality to those who are in need." Jesus told the man, "Go and do the same" (Luke 10:36–37).

It is interesting to note from this story that the two priests represented the Law and religion. Jesus was saying that neither the Law nor religion will deliver anyone from their desperate need—only the kind, generous act of hospitality by showing mercy can do that.

Preferred Method of Discipleship

When Jesus gathered with His disciples at the table for His final Passover meal, He rose from supper, took a towel, and began washing His disciples' feet (John 13:1–5). Jesus is ministering to His disciples by taking the form of a servant, demonstrating to them to be servants to one another.

After He washed their feet, He then reclined again at the table and began to talk to them about the deep issues in life. He said, "Do you know what I have done to you? You call Me Teacher and Lord; and you are right, for so I am. If I then, the Lord and the Teacher, washed your feet, you also ought to wash one another's feet. For I gave you an example that you also should do as I did to you. Truly, truly, I say to you, a slave is not greater than his master, nor *is* one who is sent greater than the one who sent him. If you know these things, you are blessed if you do them" (vv. 12–16). This teaching was followed by interactive conversation, questions and answers, clarification, and stimulating discussion—all of which took place at the table while Jesus and His disciples were eating.

For Larry and me, inviting people into our home is our preferred way to make disciples, and it seems to be the biblical way. When others come to our home to share a meal, they are not only taught through our table conversations, but Larry and I are able to model a Christian life before them. Our guests have an opportunity to view how we interact in our marriage relationship. They experience an atmosphere of love and peace and joy that permeates our environment. Our value system is lived before them, and they are able to experience a model of Christlikeness.

Several years ago, I was a guest speaker in a Detroit church. After the service ended, a young man, his wife, and preschool child introduced themselves to me. The husband reminded me that he had been a guest in our home eight years earlier with a group of men my husband had invited. With a broad grin on his face, this young father said that he and his wife based their lifestyle and their home from the two days he experienced in our home.

Apparently, several extra plates had been set at our table that weekend. Unknown to me, after every meal, this young man called his then fiancée to report his experience at the table—how it was set and what we ate. It was his first experience to be in a home like ours, demonstrating hospitality by taking in strangers. He reported that he had remembered only eating at his family table while growing up three times, and they were all holiday meals. As a young boy during those meals he thought, *I wish every day was a holiday so we could eat together.* That desire was cultivated in him while he was a guest in our home and now, with their first child, his family eats at the table regularly. They love sharing their table with others like we shared our table with him.

I mentioned earlier that hospitality overcomes the distance of strangeness and the tensions of differences. This young man was not only someone we had never met, but our ways were strange to him. Sharing an extra plate at the table relaxes our differences and begins to unify our hearts with one another.

> Hospitality overcomes the distance of
> strangeness and the tensions of differences.

Inviting someone to your home for a meal creates quality time and an opportunity for extended focused conversation. Meeting in a public place often prevents relationships from going to a deeper level. Yet setting an extra plate and meeting in your home allows conversation to go to a more personal level. Interruptions from a waiter and the intrusion of privacy in a public place keep conversation at a shallow level. The deeper level of conversation that takes place in a home, around the family table, allows a person to express honest emotions, personal pain, challenges, vulnerabilities, and current crises.

Not long ago, our dear friend Scott, who lived with our family for two years, shared with me about his experience in our home and at our table:

> I grew up in an incredible home with loving and nurturing parents. Deep down, I just knew that I was set apart and probably gifted in many areas. You could say, I was the epitome of a life untapped and undiscovered. I needed a safe place to be

launched and released. Larry and Devi's home was the perfect haven during this discovery season. Devi created a loving and hospitable environment; Larry poured his wisdom into me.

After finishing my bachelor's degree in Washington state, I sold or gave away nearly everything I owned and packed my little college car. I drove to Larry and Devi's home in Youngstown, Ohio, and stayed for two years. Throughout my time with them, I watched, listened, learned, and followed. Bottom line, I became a disciple. The principles they taught were profound. They began to change and challenge the very core of my actions and thoughts. I learned how to love people in a deeper way, how to support and disciple others.

Even though I was already saved, I needed a launching pad. I always wanted to live a life of meaning and purpose. I wanted to make a difference but had no real direction on what this actually looked like. My experiences in Larry and Devi's home, and around their table, were pivotal in helping me focus in on my calling. I am now moving forward in the right direction—doing what I feel God has created and called me to do.

Spending time in our home and around our table offered Scott a touch point for encouragement and launching pad for success. When Scott drove into our driveway on the day of his arrival, Larry greeted him with a hug and then introduced him to me for the first time. He was a stranger to me. This stranger became a friend and this friend became a relative. Scott married our granddaughter and is the father of our first great-grandchild. Little did we know that we were training our granddaughter's future husband. I'm so grateful our hearts were open to him!

Serving Others Is a Family Value

As I have mentioned, setting an extra plate at our table when I was growing up was not uncommon, neither was it uncommon for

Larry and me to set an extra plate in our home. Our two children seldom remember family dinners with only the four of us. More often than not, we sat an extra plate at the table for a guest. I made it a common practice to cook more than the four of us could eat so that at a moment's notice someone could join us for a meal. My husband loves people and often wants to bring others home with him. Because showing hospitality was a common expression of my parents, it was easy for me to provide this environment for Larry.

A distinguishing aspect of Larry's pastoral effectiveness is that he builds one-on-one relationships and trains people for improved living by inviting them into our lives to see how a godly family interacts. He models true Christianity for people in a very real way. Although our churches grew quite large, Larry never stopped inviting people into our home. We have had dozens of people live with us, and hundreds have spent several days at a time with us in our forty-five years of marriage.

This is why it was so natural and easy for me to begin the Mentoring Mansion and invite eight ladies to spend four days with me to learn about how to make their homes sanctuaries of love and havens of peace. Others often say to me, "Isn't this difficult? It is so much work to prepare meals for eight ladies three times a day for four days. That seems exhausting to me! How do you do it?" For me, mentoring is not a program I have developed; it is a lifestyle of hospitality—inviting others into my life.

The Extra Plate Has Enriched Our Lives

While preparing to speak at a conference, I was looking for a personal story that would illustrate my point. I was teaching on the importance of building memorials so the generations to come can know the goodness of God in our lives. I decided to call our son, Aaron, and ask him my question. Aaron is very conversational, thinks quickly, and easily answers questions on almost any subject. I thought this would be a quick and easy solution to my need for a personal story as I was putting the final touches on my presentation. I already had in mind the answer I wanted him to give me; I was certain that he would say exactly what fit my point. I asked him, "Aaron, what was the one thing that impacted your life the most about growing up in our home?" I was sure he would say that it was the elaborate holidays that I had prepared or the favorite meals that I had cooked for him, but he did not say that at all! He replied without hesitation, "Oh, that's easy, Mom, it was the people we had in our home!"

He went on to describe the people as he remembered them. Our strangers became his friends. "You and Dad invited ex-convicts and missionaries, scientists and preachers, and people from all races and ethnic backgrounds. Some people were very simple and others were very sophisticated. The diversity of the people you had in our home made an impression on me—each one telling their own story. Around our table, I learned lessons that I will never forget."

Truly the unique people who ate at our table have enriched our lives in many ways. Jesus said that when we set an extra plate for the least of these, it is as if Jesus Himself is sitting at our table (Matt. 25:40). His presence blessed our guests and shaped the values of our children.

Essential to Biblical Eldership

In his first letter to Timothy, the apostle Paul instructs the young pastor regarding the qualifications of an elder or overseer in the church. Showing hospitality is actually listed as a qualification for eldership along with other highly valued characteristics: "above reproach, the husband of one wife, temperate, prudent, respectable,

able to teach, not addicted to wine, gentle and uncontentious, and free from the love of money" (3:2–3).

When we married, Larry was already in full-time vocational ministry. I knew that hospitality was something I was to practice so my husband would not be disqualified to be a leader in the church. I understood that I could hinder his effectiveness by refusing to be prepared so he could bring people to our home at anytime. So I set aside a shelf in our pantry for prepared food items so I could quickly assemble meals for unexpected guests. These items were saved for emergencies and were not used for my everyday menus. For example, although I commonly made pasta sauce from scratch, in our pantry, I kept ready-made pasta sauce. I also stocked soups, puddings, brownie mix, cake mix, and so on.

Demonstrating hospitality is not the same thing as entertaining. Entertaining is inviting someone over to perform for them, showing them how well you can cook and how lovely your heirloom china is. It includes more than eating dinner and watching a movie. Rather, hospitality is an attitude of the heart—making strangers friends. Your attitude should reflect a desire to warm the heart and refresh the spirit of those who are being served from your extra plate, whether the plate is plastic, paper, or fine china. This attitude is demonstrated by everything you do and say while your guests are present, giving them your full attention.

> Demonstrating hospitality is not the same thing as entertaining. . . . Rather, hospitality is an attitude of the heart—making strangers friends.

Graceful Conversation

Conversations with your guests should be positive and uplifting. The apostle Paul instructs, "Be wise in the way you act toward outsiders; make the most of every opportunity. Let your conversation be full of grace, seasoned with salt, so that you may know how to answer everyone" (Col. 4:5–6 NIV).

I cannot think of anything more miserable than to be with a negative, complaining, grumbling person. For years, when I read this passage, I thought it meant to not grumble about inviting someone over. I would think, *Why would I invite people to my home and then complain about having them there?* That makes no sense to me. Then I realized that this passage is guiding us toward the kind of conversation that we should plan when we invite others to our table. This is an opportunity to edify and build people up. From the time they are welcomed at our door, our conversation should begin seasoning the evening as if the entire experience is a meal in itself.

I like to think of the predinner conversation as the appetizer, the beginning course of the conversation that will be served to your guests while they are with you. Scripture reminds us that when we are with people who are "outsiders," people who are not our family or closest friends, we are to take advantage of this time and maximize our opportunity to make them feel special. Ephesians 4:29 tells us, "Let no unwholesome word proceed from your mouth, but only such a word as is good for edification according to the need of the moment, so that it will give grace to those who hear."

Conversation that is seasoned with grace leads us to choose our words wisely and only say things that bring out the best in the people we are talking to. Giving grace with our words could be the same as giving favor when favor is not really deserved—saying kind words to unkind people. That's what grace does. You have the power and position as you serve your guests to improve their self-image and confidence. Scripture tells us to earnestly desire to edify and comfort others (1 Cor. 12:31). When we do this, something profound and supernatural happens in their hearts—we can prophesy what is to come to their lives—hope, destiny, love, and peace. All of this can happen when we set an extra plate and chose to focus on blessing those who are sharing our table.

> Conversation that is seasoned with grace leads us to choose our words wisely and only say things that bring out the best in the people we are talking to.

Our Sunday Dinner Experience

Inherent in practicing hospitality is demonstrating a personal value—the value of serving. Because we practiced this value at home, our children and grandchildren are involved in serving others. Their character was shaped while they participated in preparing for our Sunday dinner.

Sundays were busy days in our home. Because Larry was a full-time senior pastor, we were at the church before anyone else arrived. During our early years of ministry, we both taught Sunday school, Larry led worship, I played the organ, we rehearsed the choir, and he preached. Then we returned to the church for a Sunday evening service. The evening service was not merely a repeat of the morning service; it was a unique time of worship and Larry preached another sermon—two messages every Sunday. People who attended other churches on Sunday mornings came to our service on Sunday nights. Our building was packed with more than one thousand people. It was in this service that our hundred-voice youth choir sang. When they sang, it seemed that the roof would rise. Their worship was glorious! When church was over, it was late and the children needed to go to bed because they had school the next day. With this schedule, it would seem that our Sunday dinner would get lost in all of the responsibilities of the day. I probably would have been justified to consider myself too busy to prepare a meal and come home for dinner. However, I'm so glad that I did not rationalize this and rob my family of the lifetime memories we experienced during our Sunday dinners.

Sunday dinners require Saturday preparation. Saturdays were very important preparation days for our family. After eating breakfast at the table, our whole family (including our live-in guests) worked together to prepare the house for the weekend. The guys vacuumed the carpet and mowed the yard while the girls finished laundry, changed sheets, dusted the furniture, prepared our Sunday clothing, set the table, and did some of the meal preparation for our Sunday dinner. Everyone picked up their bedrooms and hung up any piled-up clothing. I made sure that the bathrooms were sanitized and ready for guests.

I made cleaning house fun for everyone, just like my mother made it fun for me. We made up games, dividing the rooms and running races to see who could finish first. We helped one another and always had a

---

Make Your Table a Place of Cooperation

Before the meal:

- Preparation responsibilities should be designated before the meal.

- Everyone waits for Mom to be seated before saying the mealtime prayer.

During the meal:

- Dad can begin conversation if he is home, while Mom and the oldest child serve the plates.

After the meal:

- No one individual should be assigned to clear the table alone. It is the responsibility of each person to clear his own dishes until the table is clean.

reward for the end of the morning. I know it sounds like we worked all day, but that was not so. When everyone helps, preparing the house is finished quickly.

Sunday dinner at home was a tradition that I carried from both my family and Larry's family. Lots of thought, time, and energy went in to making it a special meal. I usually served dinner in the dining room and used my best tableware. This was our big meal of the day. In the evenings, we ate a second helping of the earlier meal or snacks. We seldom ate a Sunday meal with just the four of us; Larry and I regularly filled our table. Our guest list usually included close friends as well as people we did not know very well. At church, I scanned the audience and extended an invitation to someone who may have never been honored to be invited to a pastor's home for dinner. Not only did we enrich their lives, but they also enriched ours.

Why Won't They Leave the Table?

Not long ago, a dear woman named Sherri attended a Home Mentoring Intensive at the Mentoring Mansion. Prior to coming to the mansion, she was tired and burned out. She had lost her enthusiasm. Her trip to the mansion had been arranged by her family as a birthday gift, so she had no idea what to expect.

During the four days we spent together, Sherri was very emotional. I asked her to tell me about what was going on, and she shared with me a beautiful story of the sacrifice and reward of extending hospitality to others.

> My husband and I have been self-employed custom harvesters for the last twelve years. Most people don't know what that is! We own the large pieces of machinery, called combines, required to harvest crops of grain. Some farmers have a combine or two to

harvest their own crops, others hire custom harvesters to come in and harvest their crops for them. My husband and I own several machines, trucks, and grain trailers, and we provide the workers to pull into a field and get the crops out quickly.

We return to the same farms year after year, but this is seasonal work. We start in May and end in November each year. Since we cannot offer year-round work, every season starts with new employees. Many men have come and gone—men from America, New Zealand, and even some from South Africa. We travel from state to state, we live in travel trailers, we work every day that the weather permits, and we furnish all meals (three meals a day, seven days a week). These people become family. The hours are exhausting, and we've gone months with no day off, so it's easy to get burned out.

Here's where custom harvesting and the Mentoring Mansion collide. Devi taught on the table principle, and I wept through the entire teaching. One of the comments that my husband and I have made many times regarding the workers who travel with us is, "Why won't they leave the table?" We're all exhausted; suppertime might be at midnight or one in the morning, but there they are gathered at the table. Eating, laughing, recounting the stories of the day. Lingering. I have to admit that this has sometimes been a great irritation to me. I would think, *Can't they talk when they get back to their trailer? Haven't they been together all day anyway? Good grief!*

That's why I wept. I had known these men were a ministry, but I had such a bad attitude at times. They didn't know it; I kept a smile on my face and tried to make good meals and interact kindly. I would always try to be a good hostess. The workers are so appreciative. They compliment extravagantly at times. They arrange to have family send gifts for me from their homeland, such as cookbooks, dish towels, placemats with photos of landscapes from home, favorite recipes. They've given me jewelry made from sea shells from their region, socks from their favorite teams, figurines, cards, all expressions of gratitude. How could I be so blind to the importance of my job?

I've also heard many heartbreaking stories shared by these men, most of them in their twenties. A passing comment about being left in the car all night as a child while his dad was in the pub—evidently a regular event, to give this young boy a coke and a bag of chips and leave him in the car for hours. Comments to one another about how they've dealt with the divorce of parents. When I reflect on some of the things these men have shared, I realize how profound the table had been. How many photos we've taken of birthdays that we've tried to make special because these men were so far away from home and family. Truth is, I had grown weary in doing that too. I had developed such a bad attitude. I would think, *I'm tired of going to the trouble.* I'm reflecting on a young man that quit his job abruptly this year. He was from New Zealand. In his mid-twenties. He had been drinking and gotten himself into some sort of trouble so we heard through the "rumor mill" later. He knocked on my trailer door, gave me two cup towels he'd had sent over from New Zealand, and told me he was waiting for a taxi to pick him up to take him to the airport. He gave me a hug, tears welled up in his eyes, and he told me I was the nicest person he had ever met. *How could that be?* I thought. He hardly knew me. We hadn't interacted that much. I had just cooked his meals for the last three months. I saw him (and about twenty other people) at meal time. What made him think I was so nice? Could it have been a presence other than me? Someone he didn't recognize, couldn't identify, but sensed. Someone who accepted him and loved him—the Bread of the Presence: Jesus Christ Himself.

I never said it out loud, but I used to think I had been demoted in life. I had been a professional. I spent my twenties working in the oil and gas accounting group for a major oil company in California. My husband had also been with a different oil company and gotten transferred to Kansas. Because of the transfer, I went back to college and became a registered nurse. This is the profession I left in order to help my husband do what he loves—custom harvesting. Now my duty is to be my husband's helpmate. I've worked to support him, not realizing the importance of my work. That's what God revealed to me during this teaching of the table principle. I will strive to remember that it is Jesus I cook for, and I will always invite Him to the table.

Elders, Equals, Babes

Good hospitality includes planning and preparation as well as spontaneity. Either way, your preparedness says, "I'm glad you are here." Gracious hospitality was a high value in the New Testament church. This quality is listed among essential characteristics for elders and for widows who would be supported by the church. "A widow is to be put on the list [to be supported financially] only if she is not less than sixty years old, having been the wife of one man, having a reputation for good works; and if she has brought up children, *if she has shown hospitality to strangers*, if she has washed the saints' feet, if she has assisted those in distress, and if she has devoted herself to every good work" (1 Tim. 5:9–10; emphasis added).

> Good hospitality includes planning and
> preparation as well as spontaneity.

Three of these listed qualities include acts of kindness by extending oneself as a servant: hospitality to strangers, washing the saints' feet, and assisting those in distress. Devoting yourself to every good work means that it takes work to extend yourself to others in a way that could change their lives.

A great formula for creating a guest list is to include people you can learn from (elders), people who are at a similar stage in life (equals), and people who can learn from you (babes). This type of group always is interactive, has lots to talk about, and has lots to give one another. Everyone's life is enriched when the party is over. It is very important to remember older people and include them. This makes them feel valued. Hospitality is not only for our personal pleasure, but setting the extra plate is about creating pleasure for others to enjoy.

Invite your children's neighborhood friends. Today's culture, with so many families separated by divorce, mothers who must earn a wage, and children who are home alone, fending for themselves provides a great opportunity to set an extra plate and invite your neighbor's children to stay for dinner. This gives them a nutritious meal and a healthy atmosphere that could shape their choices for their future. Their experience at your table, talking and connecting with other people, may be the only time of affirmation that they will get that day.

Invite people outside your circle of friends. We had lived in our home for five years and had never hosted a Christmas party for our neighbors. During the holidays, our time was consumed with church activities, staff parties, and choir concerts. I did not have time to plan a holiday party for neighbors and also have a party for our staff. It had been our custom to host a church staff appreciation dinner party in our home during the holidays.

This particular year, Larry and I explained to our staff that we were not giving a party for them. Rather, we wanted to extend hospitality to our neighbors. I passed out invitations door to door for a come-and-go holiday dessert party. I baked several desserts and set up a coffee bar. Everything was displayed in a creative, decorative way. Soon people began arriving—many more than we expected. They came, but they didn't go! Everyone was enjoying themselves; laughter and chatter filled the rooms along with Larry's piano concert of Christmas carols. Some of our guests were symphony chorus members, much to our surprise, so they joined in singing. Others who could hardly carry a tune joined in and created a comical duet.

Lots of extra plates were used that evening. God's presence was among us—our home was filled with His love, peace, and joy. Our neighbors connected and continued in their gatherings year after year. Everyone's hearts were warmed and refreshed. Did we all sit at the table? No. But the Bread of the Presence filled the air as we enjoyed sharing a dessert together.

Create your own party. Do you live alone? Plan to invite someone to your table at least one time per week. Maybe it will be your Friday night entertainment. Set the extra plate and make someone else's day! After dinner, play a game, watch a movie, look at photo albums, or tell your story. What a wonderful way for you to bring joy to another person. And for the evenings that you are home alone; you're not alone at all. Set your table and know that the Bread of the Presence, your wealthy Jewish husband, is right there with you.

Everyone has an extra plate, and many people would feel honored to be invited to dine from your extra plate. Begin making your guest list and your grocery list today!

Table Reflections

1. Define *hospitality* according to the Greek definition provided in this chapter.

2. How did Jesus set an example for His disciples at the Last Supper?

3. Who is valued more: the one who serves or the one who is served?

4. What does it mean to season our conversations with grace? Give an example.

5. Recall your own story of when you were impacted because someone else set out an extra plate for you.

Conclusion

THE TABLE EXPERIENCE IS the fusion of my life experience, my passion, and current research. I am convinced that something beyond our understanding happens in the human soul when we eat meals together. In this book, I have married scientific research with biblical insight to show you the transformation we experience when we eat meals together. I understand that we may have differences in our theological interpretations; this book is not meant to be a biblical commentary. But my hope is that you have gleaned a new conviction that will bring you to the table regularly with people you want a connection with.

Every human soul has its unique nuances. Each of us was uniquely formed in our mother's womb. Our personalities vary, and so do our body types. We are diverse in every way. All men are not alike, neither are all women. We do not have the same number of hairs on our heads. However, there is one thing we all share—the need to connect.

> There is one thing we all share—the need to connect.

We are uniquely and wonderfully made. As my husband often says, "I am awesome, and you are incredible!" Centuries of research continues to reveal the deep value of connection and brings light to the evolving understanding of human emotions. A recent decade of studies shows results that eating together in a positive edifying atmosphere can build personal confidence and work miracles in the human heart to stabilize emotions and create bonding.

I believe that God's heart is to connect with His creation. This is why Jesus said, "'Behold, I stand at the door and knock; if anyone hears My voice and opens the door, I will come in to him and will dine with him, and he with Me" (Rev. 3:20). As we have seen in this book, to dine with someone is to connect with that person. In other words, God is saying that He wants to connect with you.

The table experience with your spouse, family, friends, and colleagues—even your enemies—has the potential to begin bonding human hearts in a new way, a deep way that brings a spiritual connection, a bonding that life's circumstances should not break. During meals hurting hearts heal, sad hearts are made glad, depressed hearts get new vision, and divided hearts come to peace.

The table experience reveals the secret potential in each person to expand character and connection because of the presence that is among us when we eat—the Bread of the Presence, God's supernatural work accomplishing what we cannot achieve alone. The table experience bonds human relationships. Face-to-face, our hearts connect. I encourage you to set your table as an act of faith, and the supernatural, redemptive presence of the One who meets you there will do the rest.

Notes

Chapter 1—Come to the Table

1. *Yada* is the Hebrew word used in the Old Testament to refer to knowing someone in an intimate sense. For a more in-depth study of this biblical principle, see "Yada: Intimacy with God," audio single CD, available through Living Smart Resources, 330-782-5050 or www.mentoringmansion.com/resources.htm.

2. Notes taken by Devi Titus at George Barna conference, 2000. Currently, in an article entitled "Evangelical Stance on Divorce Is Changing," Adelle Banks reports that "27 percent of 'born-again' Christians have been divorced, compared with 25 percent of non-born again Americans, according to a 2007 study by the Barna Group, a California research firm." *Fort Worth Star-Telegram*, 1 March 2007, available at http://www.star-telegram.com/religion/story/504853.html. Accessed 14 March 2008.

3. Emphasis added to all scriptures in this list.

4. Edward Gibbon, "Five Basic Reasons Great Civilizations Wither and Die," *The Decline and Fall of the Roman Empire* (London: Strahan and Cadell, 1776-1789), reprinted by n.p.: Sterling Publishing Company, 1910.

5. Ibid.

6. Miriam Weinstein, *The Surprising Power of Family Meals: How Eating Together Makes Us Smarter, Stronger, Healthier, and Happier* (Hanover, NH: Steerforth Press, 2005), 1.

7. For more on Weinstein's research that eating family meals together makes us "smarter, stronger, healthier, and happier," see her Web site: www.poweroffamilymeals.com.

8. Weinstein, *The Surprising Power of Family Meals*, 145.

Chapter 2: A Place at God's Table

1. For more about the Mentoring Mansion and the Home Mentoring Intensive, see www.mentoringmansion.com.

2. Devi Titus and Marilyn Weiher, *The Home Experience: Making Your Home a Sanctuary of Love and a Haven of Peace* (Youngstown, OH: Living Smart Resources, 2006).

3. Although some Bible versions use the word *table* in Genesis 43:34, the Hebrew word *panim* is more accurately translated "from before him" (NKJV).

4. Bill Huebsch, personal interview with Miriam Weinstein, *The Surprising Power of Family Meals: How Eating Together Makes Us Smarter, Stronger, Healthier, and Happier* (Hanover, NH: Steerforth Press, 2005), 146.

Chapter 3: Setting Your Table

1. Roper Public Affairs & Media study, quoted in Jacqueline Bodnar, "The Dinner Discussion: A Perfect Opportunity to Communicate with Your Kids," *Allen Family Magazine*, January/February 2008, 9.

2. Bodnar, "The Dinner Discussion," 9.

Chapter 4: Seats of Honor

1. Some of the ideas in this section are taken from Dr. James E. Murphy's sermon "Mephibosheth: A Picture of Grace," 23 April 1998, available at http://www.faithepc.org/Sermons/1998/980823.htm. Some material for this sermon was taken from Max Lucado, *In the Grip of Grace* (Dallas: Word, 1996), 101ff. and Charles R. Swindoll, *The Grace Awakening* (Dallas: Word, 1990), 63–72.

2. Vonette Bright and Barbara Ball, *The Joy of Hospitality: Fun Ideas for Evangelistic Entertaining* (Orlando, FL: New Life, 1995), 61–62. The phrase "crumbs from your table" was added by Vonette when she told this story to a group of pastors' wives at the Global Pastor's Network conference. Used by permission.

Chapter 5: Our Daily Bread

1. Weinstein, *The Surprising Power of Family Meals*, 93.
2. Ibid.
3. Ibid., 57
4. Ibid., 91.
5. "Try It—You'll Like It! Vegetables and Fruit for Children," prepared for Kids – Go for Your Life by "Filling the Gaps," Murdoch Childrens Research Institute and Royal Children's Hospital, Melbourne, Centre of Physical Activity Across the Lifespan, and Australian Catholic University, Sydney. Available at http://www.goforyourlife.vic.gov.au/hav/articles.nsf/pages/Try_it_youll_like_it_Vegetables_and_fruit_for_children?OpenDocument. Accessed 13 March 2008.
6. Michael Pollan, *In Defense of Food: An Eater's Manifesto* (New York: Penguin, 2008), 1.
7. Ibid., 7.
8. Dr. Daniel G. Amen, "ANT (Automatic Negative Thoughts) Therapy," available at http://www.idealsoulutions.com/viewarticle.php?postid=262. Accessed 14 March 2008.
9. Dr. Phil McGraw, *Family First: Your Step-by-Step Plan for Creating a Phenomenal Family* (New York: Free Press, 2004), 125.

Chapter 6: A Table Prepared for Us

1. "Frequency of Family Meals May Prevent Teen Adjustment Problems; Teens Less Likely to Do Drugs, More Motivated in School," *ScienceDaily*, 21 August 1997. Available at http://www.sciencedaily.com/releases/1997/08/970821001329.htm. Accessed 14 March 2008.
2. Erinn Figg, "Return to the Family Meal: Eating Together Puts Communication Back on Your Menu," *Family Safety & Health*, Winter 1999, 16–18.
3. Ibid.
4. Dr. Daniel G. Amen, *Change Your Brain, Change Your Life* (New York: Three Rivers Press, 1998), 3.
5. Ibid., 44.

6. Eleanor Roosevelt, quoted on The Quotations Page, under "Classic Quotes" at http://www.quotationspage.com/quote/36354.html.

7. Amen, *Change Your Brain, Change Your Life*, 58.

8. Susan Allen, *The Unintended Journey* (Enumclaw, WA: WinePress Publishing, 2002).

Chapter 8: Passing It On

1. Alix Spiegel, "The Family Dinner Deconstructed," with Renee Montagne, *Morning Edition*, NPR News, 7 February 2008.

2. Ibid.

Chapter 10: The Extra Plate

1. James Strong, LL.D., S.T.D., *The Strongest Strong's Exhaustive Concordance of the Bible* (Zondervan Publishing House, 2001), s.v. "hospitality."

About the Author

DEVI TITUS IS AMONG America's recognized Christian conference speakers. Devi came to the attention of women nationwide in 1978, when she founded and edited *Virtue* magazine, a Christian alternative to secular women's magazines. For this work, she received the Superior Performance Award by the Washington Press Women's Association.

In this decade, she created the Mentoring Mansion, developed and published *The Home Experience—Making Your Home a Sanctuary of Love and a Haven of Peace,* a stunning 275-page coffee table book and curriculum for personal or group mentoring. She serves as president of Global Pastors' Wives Network, founded by Vonette Bright, co-founder of Campus Crusade for Christ.

She has partnered with her husband, Larry, in ministry for more than forty-five years, establishing five churches. In 1992, Devi and Larry founded Kingdom Global, which relationally mentors, resources, and releases the vision of global leaders. Devi's passionate and innovative approach to life creates new venues to help women reach their full potential.

Devi and Larry have two adult children, six grandchildren, and two great-grandchildren.

RESOURCE CENTER
for Devi Titus products

Books, CD, and DVD series are available at:

www.LivingSmartResources.com

Another Related Book Created By Devi Titus To Order:

THE HOME EXPERIENCE—Making Your Home a Sanctuary of Love and a Haven of Peace

This 275-page, full-color coffee table book is both motivating to read and a mentoring curriculum to use.

Each chapter is followed by a reflection study guide, and the book also has a companion DVD series of the authors teaching the contents of most chapters. This enables you to invite friends to your home and give them home experiences to make their own homes places of love and peace. In this way, a revolution can begin to reclaim the dignity and sanctity of the home.

THE HOME EXPERIENCE includes essential principles and vital relationship skills, giving you the tools to live a loving, peaceful life. From personality styles to home cleaning and organizing, Devi Titus shares her passion and experience to assist you in making your home experience and table experience awesome joys.